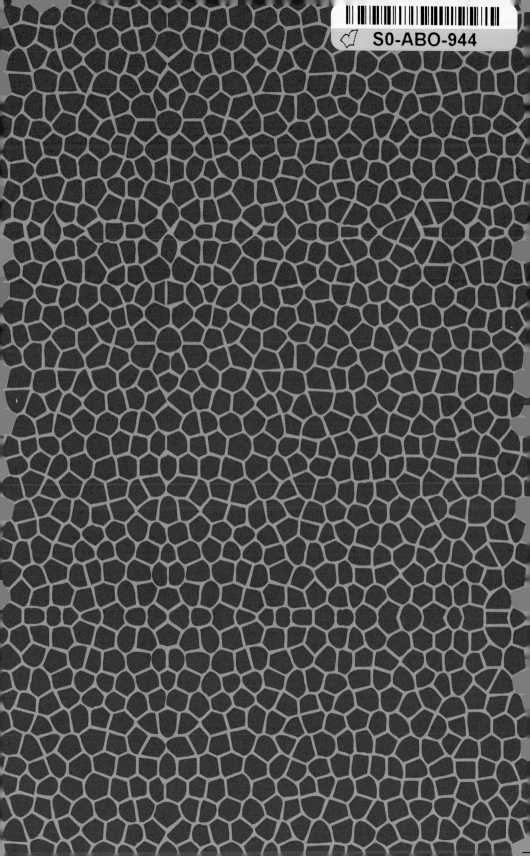

Journals
of Faith

MOSAICA PRESS

Journals *of* Faith

Cancer,
Commitment
& Hope

Ricki Lieber Simon, PhD
Ely S. Simon, MD, *z"l*

Published by Mosaica Press, Inc.
www.mosaicapress.com
info@mosaicapress.com

Table of Contents

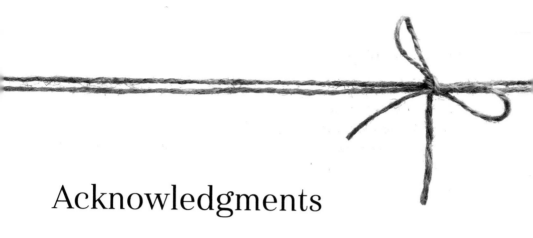

Acknowledgments

This book started as two personal journals, but it emerged from there as one entity through the efforts of many people.

I would like to first thank the wonderful people at Mosaica Press, and more specifically Rabbi Doron Kornbluth for an excellent editing job, Mrs. Rayzel Broyde for her creative graphic design, Mrs. Sherie Gross for her thorough copyediting, and Rabbi Yaacov Haber for his encouragement and input. I would like to thank the entire staff for their professionalism and support. It was truly a positive experience working with them.

I would like to thank my parents, Asher and Nechama Lieber, for their consistent faith in me and encouragement, and of course for their tremendous love, which I have always felt, but especially so at this time.

I would like to thank Ely's parents, Bob and Lee Simon, who have always been and continue to be supportive in every way. Even in their grief, they always make sure that we and everyone else in the family are taken care of. They embraced me from day one, and they continue to do so unconditionally. I have no words to thank them.

I would like to thank each of my children, for rallying around me when I most needed them. Each one has contributed to my healing in his or her own way.

I would like to thank Ely's children for their encouragement and support, both during the time of the illness and afterwards.

As is clear from some of the descriptions in the book, our community in Modiin was truly a bedrock, and I would like to thank the wonderful people of our *shul*, Choshen Modiin, for supporting us in countless ways during this trying time.

Most importantly, I would like to thank Hashem for all of the blessings He has given me in life—listing some of them would be too limiting and would not even begin to capture the true essence of what He has given me.

Love is a living breathing thing.

It doesn't die.

It changes form. It morphs.

But it is as real as anything physical.

I can sometimes feel it, pulsating, moving, enveloping.

Not logical, sometimes unexpected,

it is a gift from God.

Introduction

Meet Ely

DECEMBER 31, 2018/ 23 TEVET 5779

ONCOLOGY WARD, BEILINSON HOSPITAL (PETACH TIKVAH, ISRAEL)

There is nothing like being told that you have a life-threatening illness to make you focus on living.

In this book, I share my thinking and insights that help me cope, and even thrive, during this difficult time in my life.

As I am writing this, I am in the midst of a series of treatments to rid my body of a malignant neoplasm; in common language—cancer. This came out of nowhere, as I have always led a healthy lifestyle. Indeed, throughout my fifty-five years, I have not had any chronic illnesses, and I have hardly needed any medications at all.

However, I recently noticed a lump growing on the side of my neck. A few weeks later, after some medical investigation, I was informed of the serious nature of this tumor and its related damage that was already taking place. These details are important only to emphasize that I am yet in the early stages of the recommended treatments. As I write this, the outcome is unknown, and my future is uncertain.

I am by nature a highly analytical and rational thinker. My schooling has taught me the rigors of the sciences, engineering, and medicine, as well as the ordered thought needed to study Talmud. Professionally, I am a clinical neurologist and brain scientist, and I enjoy dabbling in innovative and entrepreneurial enterprises. In addition, over the past decade, I have made a concerted effort to expand my education to include matters of the mind, emotions, cognitive psychology, decision-making, and how our minds define us as moral human beings. These studies have also expanded my horizons in classical Jewish thinking to include an important body of literature that was largely omitted from my earlier education—texts organized to help explain the basic spiritual foundations of our existence as people in this world, our relationships with ourselves, with others, and with God. These latter perspectives, delivered from different angles from different texts authored over the past millennium by Jewish luminaries, such as Maimonides, Rabbi Moshe Chaim Luzzatto, Rabeinu Bahya Ibn Paquda, and Rabbi Samson Raphael Hirsch, have largely provided me with healthy viewpoints on the meaning and purpose of life. Ultimately, this is what is helping me now while dealing with the present existential threat to my life.

My ability to cope at any given time is solely a reflection of the ongoing battle between positive and negative thoughts within my head. My attitude results from how I choose to manage my thoughts and to interpret the events unfolding around me. How well I manage these thoughts ultimately determines how much or how little suffering I experience, both mentally and physically.

The topic of this book is how I am managing my thoughts. My purpose in sharing these insights is that they may help inspire others to find their own paths to healthy thinking in the difficult situations that they—indeed, all of us—face in life.

This book is a personal reflection, and is not intended as a philosophical, psychological, sociological, or theological treatise. In it, I let my thoughts flow, unhampered by having to conform to the opinions of scholars in the respective fields. I do not pretend to master classical philosophy, other religions, or general non-Jewish ideas. My personal orientation is based firmly on Jewish tradition, although there, too, I am not a scholar.

I have chosen to style this book as my personal journey—an analytical reflection interleaved with diary entries that I have been logging as spontaneously recorded thoughts from the day that this chapter of my life started just over a month ago.

Meet Ricki

JANUARY 28, 2019/ 2 SHEVAT 5779
5:30 A.M., HOME (MODIIN, ISRAEL)

I am writing this just two days before Ely is scheduled to undergo major surgery. Over the last two months, I have been writing down some of the emotions and thoughts that have accompanied me through this difficult time. I am now getting used to the idea of sharing these thoughts in public.

By nature, I am a private person. I am not accustomed to sharing life events publicly, or outwardly expressing strong emotion, even at family gatherings. I like to observe from the sidelines rather than put myself into the thick of things. People may think of me as somewhat reserved, not prone to speaking up.

However, a few things have changed over the last few years. For one thing, I have recently undergone training to be a life coach.

Let me explain: For the last nineteen years, I have been working as a patent agent, mostly in the field of medical devices. This is highly technical and analytical work, and mostly involves sitting in front of a computer, with occasional human interaction in the form of client meetings. My educational background includes a Ph.D. in biomedical engineering, although I always had a love of Jewish learning and received a bachelor's degree in Jewish Studies as well.

Still, although I am somewhat reserved, I enjoy interacting with people, I get along just fine in social environments, and when appropriate, I can get up in front of a crowd and comfortably speak in public. I started to feel the gap between who I really am and the work that I have been doing professionally more and more acutely over the last few years. I also started to wonder what my contribution to society was and whether I could do more to help people. It was then that I discovered life coaching.

Without really knowing what I was getting myself into, I signed up for a course to learn how to be a life coach. Little did I know that the course itself was a type of group therapy. We were a group of about twenty women, and slowly over the year or so that we were together, we started to share parts of our lives with people who just months before had been total strangers. We learned how to listen, to empathize, to ask relevant questions, and to get down to the heart of what makes us human. This course opened up a whole world for me; it unlocked my ability—and even my need—to identify my emotions more and to share them and other powerful thoughts with others. Despite this, I am still shy about sharing my feelings with others, even those who are close to me.

All of that is now starting to change as well, with this new life situation that I find myself in. As I have been writing short pieces over the last two months, I have shared a few of them with close family. The feedback has been very positive, and I realized that I have something to say that could potentially help people in coping with many varied challenging life situations.

Sharing these thoughts helps me as well. I have recently expanded my circle to outer rings of friends and family. So if my initial sharing of thoughts could be compared to putting my toe in the water, and the expansion of my circle is akin to putting my legs in the water, this book is now a head-first dive off the high board.

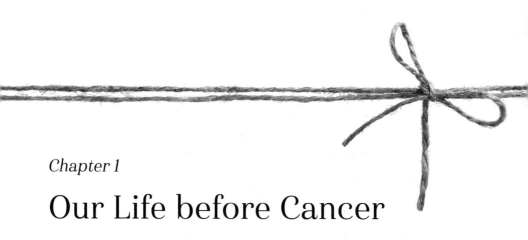

Chapter 1

Our Life before Cancer

Ely and I shared a profound life together. This was a second marriage for both of us, the first ones having ended in divorce. From the start, our relationship was based on a deep connection and personal growth. When we married in December 2010 (Tevet 5771), Ely had four daughters from his previous marriage, three of whom were married with children: Deena (married to Yakir), Rivka (married to Chaim), Yael (married to Shiloh), and Meira. I had two daughters and three sons from my previous marriage: Yafi, Avishai, Zaky, Eitan, and Renana. In October 2011/ Tishrei 5772, Ely and I were also blessed with a baby daughter, Tamar.

Life was challenging in the early years of our marriage, having to navigate the varied needs of children and grandchildren, while trying to build our combined life. But no matter how challenging it was, we always found a way to understand our difficulties in a greater context. We worked together to understand why these challenges were presented to us, how they related to our personal growth and to the overall plan that God must have for our family, and we tried to make our decisions based on truth and intuition.

During the entire time of our marriage, we worked on ourselves through introspection and through the study of Jewish sources. We used our challenges to grow, to develop, and to start understanding our purpose in the world.

During the eight years of our marriage, we lived in three different places, we celebrated two additional marriages of our children (Meira to

Yoav, and Yafi to Amiad), welcomed the addition of multiple grandchildren, and suffered through job loss as well as other difficult challenges. A lot of life was squeezed into eight years, not to mention the leaps and bounds that our inner lives went through during that time.

Three years ago, in June 2016 (Sivan 5776), we settled down in Modiin, and began to seriously plan our life's work. We had settled into our married life, the family dynamics began to become easier, and we talked at length about a multitude of ideas of how we could help people, together. Just before Ely was diagnosed, he had put together a team of people to form what he called the "Brain Health Center," which was intended to be a virtual clinic for brain health, with integrated care coordinated between many different professionals, including neurologists, geriatricians, psychologists, life coaches, occupational and physical therapists, nutritionists, physical trainers, sleep coaches, and more. The idea was that (with a dose of modesty) each professional would realize that no one person has all the answers, and that an integrated approach to brain health would provide far better care than the current model of each person working alone. In addition, the focus would be on health and preventative care, and the organization would include lectures, workshops, and activities for the public.

In truth, the idea "behind the idea" was that the key to brain health is healthy thinking. I had just finished training as a life coach, and the plan was to incorporate my life coaching into the holistic brain health center, wherein my practice would be centered on Jewish thinking in particular. Ely and I spent countless hours discussing the types of activities that might be included, and we spent countless hours discussing the types of thinking that might help people in their lives. We always focused on incorporating many of the Jewish sources that we had learned and continued to learn, together and separately. This would be an authentically Jewish, Torah-based, medically advanced holisitic approach to the brain and the mind. We were excited.

However, just as we were about to launch the center, our lives were disrupted. We had to put our plans on hold and focus on medical care for Ely. In a sense, this new life situation now took over and took us away from our concrete plans. But in a different sense, we were suddenly thrust into a situation in which all of the theoretical ideas and "nice" thoughts that we had had until now were tested on us, in real life. Ely and I were very aware of the importance of chronicling our thought patterns during this difficult time, and he expressed to me many times during the course of his illness that perhaps it is for this very reason that he became ill—to be able to experience and express first-hand the thoughts and ideas that we had been working on for so long.

Chapter 2

Pre-Diagnosis:
How It All Began

On November 16, 2018 (8 Kislev 5779), Ely went for an ultrasound to check out something that he had been feeling in his neck for about two weeks. It was a Friday morning, and I was on the phone with my sister, planning when we could spend a Shabbat together. At the time, it seemed like a regular Friday morning.

NOVEMBER 19, 2018/ 11 KISLEV 5779

Ricki Has It Only Been Three Days?

I am sitting in my living room, grappling with a difficult life situation, and I decided to write down what I am going through and how I am dealing with it.

On Friday, my husband, Ely, went for an ultrasound to see what was causing what seemed like an enlarged lymph node in his neck. Just the day before, he had been at the dentist, who assured him that an infection in his tooth could be the cause. Because of that, I was not particularly worried.

He came back close to an hour later, with a grave look on his face. It's not good, he said. Bracing myself, I asked him what he meant. He told me that there is a mass there, with necrotic (i.e., dead) tissue, and that the mass is impinging on the veins and arteries in his neck. In fact, he said, the jugular vein on one side is thrombosed—that is, totally blocked from blood supply—and the carotid artery on the same side (the major source of blood to the brain) might be in danger. The doctor ordered blood tests, a full body CT scan,[1] and a biopsy.

Just like that, our life has changed.

We don't yet know what it is, how serious it is, and what it all means, but nonetheless our life has changed.

We spent all day Friday and Shabbat grappling with this news. It was very surreal. We started talking about what things are important to accomplish in the time we have left—whether it is a short time or fifty years. The sudden, very real possibility that his life might be in danger led to a cascade of actions and thoughts.

On Sunday, we decided to drive out to see his parents and let them know what was going on. Even though we still didn't have too much information, we felt it was important to involve them at this stage. His mother said that not knowing was the most difficult part. We did what we could to push the tests forward.

I have been oscillating between thoughts of worry, sadness, and begging God to keep him safe. I have absolute belief that God is involved in our lives and in everything that happens to us.

I know in my heart that God is good.

But what does that mean? Does that mean that bad things can't happen to me? As long as I am good? Clearly that is not true. Just look at the story of Iyov. Iyov's lesson was that he thought he knew how the system worked, or how it was supposed to work, but he was wrong. He had to have the *anavah* and the *bitachon* to understand that in truth, he doesn't really get it. That his assumptions might not be true. That just because you are a good person doesn't mean that you will have a good life. God is good, and there is reward and punishment, but how that applies to individual circumstances in our life is not clear at all.

---

1   A CT (computed tomography) scan uses X-ray measurements taken from different angles to compute an image of the scanned area in the body.

I also am very aware that everything that happens to us is for a reason. Jews are taught—and I believe—that there is no randomness in the events that we are faced with, and that the trials we are given are there for us to grow into who we need to be in the world.

But with all of that, I can't help thinking: not this, God, please not this. I need Ely. I need him in the world with me as we go through our life journey. We are "supposed" to go through it together.

But what if I am wrong? Maybe we are not "supposed" to go through it together. Maybe this is some kind of punishment, or maybe it is somehow important for the greater good. I find myself trying to be completely reliant on God and His decisions, knowing we are in good hands. But I don't know how—at the same time—to pray for what seems (to us) to be a good outcome and yet accept whatever outcome there will be. Also, do I have a say in this? Is his health dependent on my handling the situation right?

Today, Monday, both of us woke up with disturbing thoughts that the testing is taking too long. That we need to push things forward somehow. But then we sat down for our morning coffee, and Ely explained to me why it is actually good that we don't know yet, and that we need to go with the flow.

What came out of this conversation are the following insights, which are allowing me to deal with the uncertainty and the worry in a much better way.

1. *Bitachon*—**Trust.** A physical example will help: There is a principle in physics which, while completely non-intuitive, has been proven to be true. Until an electron is observed, its location is not just unknown, it is actually not fixed. That is, there is a possibility space, and the electron is located in the entirety of the possibility space at the same time. However, once that electron is observed, its location is fixed and can no longer be in any of the places that it might have been in before the observation took place. It is a fascinating concept, which seems to fly in the face of logic—yet is proven to be scientifically true.

We, too, are at a point of uncertainty. We don't know what this mass is, whether it is benign or malignant, whether it is growing or shrinking, what the prognosis is, what the possible treatments are, etc. The more information we collect, the more the possibility space will shrink.

But—we need to always remember that as we get more information, and the possibility space shrinks, we still will not *know* the outcome until the very end of the journey.

This relates directly to *bitachon*. The same God that put this mass there has the power to make it go away. No matter what the medical establishment tells us, we cannot fall into the trap of thinking we *know* what is going to be. Because that false "knowing" can be a self-fulfilling prophecy. It can fix the results, and that may not be what we want or what is right. So we have to do what we can to produce a good outcome, including praying, but we can't push the process forward any faster than we can, and we have to calmly go step by step. As things become more clear, we have to remember, always, that there is one Being who determines the outcome.

Also, we always need to remember that the outcome will be Good. Good with a capital "G". There is an ultimate good, which doesn't always seem to match up with events in our lives. But in reality, it always matches up with what is right for the Divine plan. This thought makes me calm, and when I really grab it, I feel enveloped by the love that Hashem has for us.[2]

2. Meaning and purpose. This event has already forced us to be razor sharp in our focus about what to contribute to the world. If you had a limited time to live (which we all do), would you think to yourself: what can I **get** from this world? Or what can I **give** to this world? This makes all the difference in how you

---

2   The terms "Hashem" and "God" are used interchangeably throughout.

decide to spend your time. And since we are sitting with a potentially crushing object on the jugular, we really feel the urgency in
completing our tasks in this world.

This has caused us to think very carefully about what to spend
our time on—and what not to spend our time on. Each of us has
almost an infinite number of choices about what to do with our
time. What we decide will determine how much we have used our
most precious resource in the right way.

This has also caused us to introspect and to try to get more
clarity on who we are. For example, until now, Ely thought that
his role was at least partially to educate people about brain health.
Well, it may be that that is not his unique contribution to the
world. It turns out he has lots of thinking and ideas behind big
life questions, such as *bitachon*. We also came onto the fact that
he does not need to work on ways to get people to hear what he
has to say. He needs to just say it, articulate it, perhaps teach it to
educators. To put it out there in the world. The rest can happen
without him. His critical role is becoming more clear.

My role is becoming clearer as well. I see the struggles that I
have grappled with until today, and now even more sharply, the
current struggles that I am going through, as a springboard to
help people cope with life situations through the lens of *bitachon*—and Torah. I need to develop my ideas and to test them
out with real people in the real world.

3. Gratitude. I told Ely this morning that I am thankful he
is here with me today. This is the way we need to live. Every
day. *Dayeinu.*

Refuah sheleimah l'Eliyahu Shmuel ben Leah

NOVEMBER 20, 2018/ 12 KISLEV 5779

Ely Perspective

Today is November 20th, 2018 (12 Kislev 5779). Ricki and I
are going through a very trying time. I have learned that I have

a mass in my neck and the doctors are concerned. They want me to go through tests. We're going to be having a needle aspiration biopsy on Thursday, and that will be giving us information about what this is, what it will likely turn out to be, and what treatment will be recommended.

The challenge is to maintain the right perspective. We are concerned, but we do not know what it is, and it is entirely in God's hands. It could turn out to be benign, it could turn out to be malignant, it could turn out to be treatable, and it could turn out to be fatal. We don't know. That uncertainty is part of life and that's fine. That's just the way it is. There are always risks and danger. We just happen to be aware of a particular danger at this moment.

Our total trust in Hashem and His doing what's ultimately good will give us the right perspective going forward. We will use every moment of the time we have left to the best that we can, to the greatest enjoyment, to fulfill our mission, and to be close to our loved ones. That should always be the approach in our life and should have nothing to do with an imminent danger, so thank God that we're able to focus.[3]

NOVEMBER 20, 2018/ 12 KISLEV 5779

Ricki Worry Creeps In

It's amazing how worry creeps in. Despite everything I wrote yesterday, in the middle of the night I found myself worrying. My thought patterns got tripped up at three points:

---

3   Comment by Ely at a later date: *"Bitachon"* is the code word for the core belief that I can totally trust in God—His constant presence, His caring, His love, and His goodness. As will become clear, for me, these facts and perceptions are as real as the bottle of water in front of me and the computer on which I am typing. They are as real as the facts of nature, and as dependable as the sun rising and setting each day. Indeed, the seemingly random variations in the weather patterns and natural processes can potentially leave me with uncertainty about the weather conditions on a given hour, but my understanding of God's providence allows me to place my full trust in the knowledge that the overall plan is purposeful and good.

One: It is clear to me now that we needed this stimulus to move us out of our complacency. And it is also clear that there is a tendency to return to complacency when things seem OK. So I started worrying that we might "need" this to be bad news in order to keep ourselves focused on important things. But that is the wrong conclusion. If we know the weak spot (i.e., when things are good, we have a tendency to release our firm grip), then the conclusion is that we should work on correcting that tendency. Make sure it doesn't happen. Keep working at it.

Two: I got myself into the "what if" cycle. The "what if" cycle is a total dead end. We often find ourselves going there when the outcome is not known, and we think we can "think through" what will be. I found myself thinking very negative "what if" thoughts in the middle of the night. That is not only pointless, but also destructive. If I think about negative events, then I just may be consolidating that event as an actuality, which is certainly something I don't want to do. It's sort of like looking at the tree on the ski slope—the more you think to yourself "don't hit it, don't hit it," the more likely it is that you will actually hit the tree.

Three: I thought I figured it out. My logical brain starting leading me in a certain direction, and all of my figuring did not lead to a good conclusion. When will I get it through my thick skull that I don't have all the answers, and that my logic may not even be right or true? There is a Creator here, who is driving the process and controlling the outcomes. My focus needs to be on the job that we need to do. Right now. Without worry, without diversions.

Again, I am filled with gratitude for what I have.

NOVEMBER 21, 2018/ 13 KISLEV 5779

Ricki Focusing on the Work

It really is quite incredible. The more we focus on the work we have to do in this world, the less we worry about the medical situation. We just have to do what we have to do, for as long as we are able. *B'ezrat Hashem*, we will be *zocheh* to continue to do our work for many years.

I find that I am not thinking about the lump or the diagnosis too much and I am not worrying. I am just jumping into action. And by the way, part of that action is at a deeper level. Getting closer to Ely, remembering all that Hashem has done for us, having gratitude every minute, realizing that our whole story and our very existence is at another level altogether. I am feeling good and calm and ready to do my part, with love.

Chapter 3

The Day of the Diagnosis

We were told that the type of biopsy needed in this case was an ultrasound guided needle biopsy, and that it was important to have it done by an expert doctor, not just a technician. We were led to Dr. Maya Cohen at Herzliya Medical Center with very high recommendations. Indeed, our experience with Dr. Cohen was very positive. We felt that she was highly professional as well as caring, and she insisted that the pathology report be done immediately and that we should not leave until we receive the results. After a full morning of tests and waiting, she called us into her office.

NOVEMBER 22, 2018/ 14 KISLEV 5779

Ely Positive Outlook

I spend a lot of time with my patients after examining them and reviewing their symptoms, telling them what's wrong or what's not wrong. Ultimately, my goal is to work with their attitudes to improve their outlook—that they are essentially healthy people and should have a positive attitude toward life and living, rather than focus on their impairment, physical or otherwise. Many people are drawn down by poor mood, depression, or the sense that they are sick—that their ability to experience life and to enjoy life is limited. But indeed, that's their mental state, not the physical state itself. Even if I have patients who have had brain tumors or bleeds in their head, multiple sclerosis, or other serious neurological diseases, what matters most to their ability to live is their attitude.

That's what's going on here, as well, with me. I'm simply living the same way that I've been talking to my patients.

There's something going on inside me, there's a growth of some sort. We don't know exactly what it is and to what extent it's there and what danger it poses, but it's clearly something. Still, the growth doesn't define me. The illness shouldn't define me. The medical procedures shouldn't define me. It's my state of mind and my attitude and the way I choose to think that defines me.

I'm going to continue living. I'm going to continue enjoying life. If anything, this puts a very sharp focus on the importance of living every day to the fullest, and I'm going to continue to nurture relationships, to invest in the future of my family and all the projects that I'm working on and keep a positive outlook.[1]

NOVEMBER 22, 2018/ 14 KISLEV 5779

Ricki   Shock

No matter how prepared we thought we were, it was still a total shock.

Cancer.

My legs were shaking after we heard—completely involuntarily.

We don't know yet how bad it is. We are praying that this is curable, and that we will live together for many, many years.

---

1   Comment by Ely at a later date: "The importance of a positive outlook cannot be overstated. I find that my physical symptoms are highly sensitive to my psychological state. In turn, my psychological state is highly dependent on my focus on the technical matters of my diagnosis and its treatment. The more the disease becomes the topic of discussion and speculation, the more I am placed into a situation of pointless worrying. I say 'pointless' because these are negative thoughts that do not serve a purpose, and rather cause anxiety and doubt."

I am trying to keep my *bitachon*. It was strong this morning. So strong that I really wasn't worried. There is no room for worry when you fill your thoughts with your job in this world. And we are really getting clarity on that. Just this morning, we started talking about starting to share some of our ideas with the world. We have so much to say; we have been building and growing and sharing ideas for years and years. But until now, it has been between the two of us. And we realized that it is time for these ideas to be brought into the world.

So my mind was totally occupied by those thoughts this morning. Even on the way to the biopsy. Even at the clinic as we waited for the results.

It's so strange. The whole world looks different now. We came back to Modiin, and the streets look different, the people look different. But really, what has changed? Don't we already know that life is fragile, and that we have to use it to the best of our ability? Don't we already know that our time here is limited, whether it's 5, 30, 50, 80, or even 120 years?

But still.

This was a real blow.

I now have to gather back my strength and walk hand in hand with Ely. I know we are up to the task. I also know that this is all from Hashem. That is the most comforting thought that I can have.

I also know that my time with Ely is precious, and we will appreciate every moment together, never taking anything for granted.

I pray that Hashem gives us the strength that we need to deal with this in the right way, that He continue to guide us, and that He gives us enough time and insight to really do whatever it is that we are supposed to do in this world.

NOVEMBER 22, 2018/ 14 KISLEV 5779

Ricki Thought Tracks

Ely likes to describe thoughts as trains riding on tracks. If you've ever experienced different modes of thinking, you'll know that that's a really good analogy. I sometimes find myself in a certain mode that never leads to a good feeling. I either overthink or worry about a situation. I am fixated on "solving" it rather than accepting it for what it is right now, or digesting it from different angles. But when I manage to get myself onto a different track, let's call it the "relaxed thinking" route, I find that my stress level goes down, and I am able to be happy even in the face of challenging situations.

How do I make this switch? Well, first I needed to lay down the new tracks, which is a process that I have been going through for several years. My brain used to automatically go into what I like to call "planning mode," where I can figure everything out, where I can mull over pros and cons, and where I can rehash and worry. I also had a tendency to connect dots that weren't necessarily there—a skill which may sometimes be useful in solving puzzles (or other games) but which can sometimes lead to overconfidence or serious errors in sizing up and dealing with a situation.

The new tracks were laid slowly but surely, through a process of remembering to stop and pay attention, to look to God for guidance, and to recognize emotions rather than rely purely on seemingly logical thoughts. In truth, my tendency is still to go straight into "planning mode" when I am faced with a difficult situation, but if I stop and remember to switch tracks, I can get onto a much better way of thinking, which not only helps me think through things in a more holistic way, but which also makes me feel much more relaxed and calm and reduces my stress level greatly.

The basis for the "relaxed mode" track in my life is three-fold: *Bitachon*, knowing that I am here for a greater purpose, and gratitude for what God has given me.

- The *bitachon* comes from knowing, with absolute knowledge, that (a) Hashem is in charge and (b) Hashem is Good. These two points don't necessarily come easily to everyone, but I have been developing them in a stronger and stronger way over the years. Hashem is *always* there and is *always* Good. Not just sometimes. The same Hashem that gave me Ely and beautiful healthy children and so much good also gave me some difficult situations to manage.
- Which leads me to my second pillar—knowing that I am here for a greater purpose. I try to look at all of my challenges as just that. Challenges. Challenges help us grow and make us into better versions of ourselves. I have no doubt that I have been brought into this world for a reason and that all of my collective experiences make my role in this world more effective (or will in the future).
- And finally, the gratitude. No matter what is happening, there is always room for gratitude. Not just a little room, but vast open spaces that have never been tread before. We should never ever take for granted what we have, least of all our very breaths that we take every day—thousands and thousands of them.

The trick is to stay on these thought tracks as much as possible, so that they can continue to become stronger and more automatic. It requires constant effort.

Chapter 4

How Bad Is It?

On the day of the diagnosis, we knew it was cancer. We also knew that the cancer did not originate in the lymph nodes; this was known because the type of cell that was identified was a squamous cell, which generally originates in soft tissue and does not originate in the lymph node. We were told that the next steps would be a series of tests to investigate the primary source of the cancer and the extent of the spread. This was on a Thursday. The following days looked like this:

On Friday, Ely underwent a root canal (we were told to make sure all dental work was completed before any treatments could begin).

On Sunday, we met with a team of Ear Nose Throat (ENT) surgeons at Beilinson Hospital in Petach Tikvah who specialize in head and neck cancers. They searched for the primary source of the cancer, and the only thing they found was a very small, almost negligible, lesion on Ely's tongue.

On Monday morning, we returned to Beilinson for a biopsy of the tongue. On Monday afternoon, we drove to Ashdod for a PET-CT, which is a very sensitive test for cancer cells throughout the body.[1] After the PET-CT, we drove back to Beilinson to deliver the disk so that the team

---

1   PET-CT stands for Positron Emission Tomography-Computed Tomography. In short, this is a combined diagnostic test, wherein both the metabolic activity (provided by the "PET"), which gives an indication of what biochemical processes are happening in the body, and imaging (provided by the "CT"), which gives a picture or a scan of the body, are used to give a more complete picture of what is going on and where any tumor activity might be.

of ENT surgeons could review it with the Oncology staff the following morning at their weekly "tumor board."

On Friday, we went to Shaarei Tzedek hospital in Jerusalem for an MRI (magnetic resonance imaging), a test that the surgeons insisted was critical for the surgery they would likely have to perform.

On Monday, we were called into Beilinson to discuss with the doctors what they had found and what they recommended as the treatment plan.

What a week and a half that was!

NOVEMBER 23, 2018/ 15 KISLEV 5779

Ricki   Why Is It Always about Me? – a Little Dry Humor

Ely has a hard time thinking that he needs to be taken care of. "Why is it always about me?" he asked. "You should also get some attention." I started to say, "Don't worry about me right now" or something of the sort. But he interrupted and said, "No, really, just tell me what doctor you want to see, and I'll make sure to take you there."

NOVEMBER 23, 2018/ 15 KISLEV 5779

Ricki   What Do We Need from Our Loved Ones?

You are probably wondering how to approach this difficult reality—and how to interact with us. I will try to give you a little insight into how we are thinking about this and what we need from you.

I'll start by explaining what we don't need. That, I can say in one word: negativity. This includes doubts and fears. Of course, it is totally normal to have doubts and fears, but we ask that you keep that out of the conversation with us. It only serves to feed into our own doubts and fears. Included in this category are excessive medical questions. We are taking the approach that we will not get sucked into the vortex of asking all the "what if" questions, searching frantically on the Internet for answers, or hearing statistical probabilities. We will of course follow the medical path that is deemed most correct or optimal for the situation, but we will not dwell on that aspect.

So what do we need from you? As much positivity as possible. To be clear, we do not mean false positivity such as "don't worry, everything will be fine." We mean what I am now calling "substantive positivity."

What is "substantive positivity"? Essentially, when you realize that your life is limited (and again, all of ours are, but we normally don't give that too much thought), you can take that fact in one of two directions.

- You can shut down and say "What's the use"?
- You can embrace life with so much more vitality and meaning than it ever had.

If you choose the second path, if you choose to focus on the blessings, the relationships with loved ones, the purpose and meaning, and the connection with God, then not only is your time much more effective, your attitude and disposition become positive as well.

This is the way we are approaching this challenge. We are much more focused, much more appreciative, and much more alive than we were just a week ago. We hope that you can join us in those positive thoughts.

And finally, of course, we want your *tefillot*, your love, and your hugs.

NOVEMBER 25, 2018/ 17 KISLEV 5779

Ricki Roller Coaster

This is really a roller coaster of emotions.

Every once in a while, the reality of it slips in. Like in *shul* on Shabbat, when Ely received a *Mi Sheberach*. Or today, when we met with the surgeon, and he spoke in a matter-of-fact way about the next job of finding the primary tumor.

This morning, though, we were in a very high place. A place where the facts sort of faded into the background, and the main story was about our climbing higher. We were feeling relaxed, at one with the will of Hashem, in a place where our *tefillot* could have an influence. Here is the prayer we came up with:

> *Hashem, may it be Your will that Ely should live, that he should live in a way in which we are able to do our avodat Hashem, able to think and create, and that we walk hand in hand with Your plan for us.*

A little later, I had the realization that it is not enough to be accepting of Hashem's will; we must be in a place where we feel His love and where we feel tremendous love for Him and for all He has given us.

NOVEMBER 27, 2018—19 KISLEV 5779

Ricki Whirlwind

It has been a whirlwind few days. We are really getting super-fast care, and we are so grateful for that. I am tired today because of the almost non-stop running around. But we have a little break now, and it's time to regroup.

The tricky part is to stay focused and positive. We can't get sucked down into the medical details, and we certainly can't go into "what if" mode. It is hard, but we are largely succeeding. How?

By focusing on life, on living this life to the fullest. By focusing on all the good things. Life is precious, and it is in sharper focus than ever before.

NOVEMBER 28, 2018—20 KISLEV 5779

Ricki Thinking Positive

Why is it so hard to stay up there? We had a great morning, working on our ideas, planning and forging ahead. But then when Ely left the house, dark thoughts started weaving their way in. I got tired and had to nap for a bit. I started to worry, to fear the worst. I tried to stop myself, but it was hard to pick myself back up. When Ely came home, he knew that I had not been doing so well. We talked it through, and I asked him how it is that he doesn't have any down moments? He explained that his idea of thinking positive is not the same as others. Others use that term to mean that we should continue to believe and hope that everything will be fine. But the problem with that is that if there are glitches along the way, if there is any bad news, everything falls apart—the hope, the *bitachon,* and the positive outlook.

He explained that what he means by thinking positive is to focus on life. To enjoy every moment. To use our time in the best way possible. And that can only be good.

NOVEMBER 29, 2018/ 21 KISLEV 5779

 How I Keep a Positive State of Mind

First of all, let me explain what I mean by "positivity." I mean that I am living in the best way that I can, and able to do the things that I feel I need to do and to enjoy life. I do not mean what a lot of people mean by "positivity," which is that everything will turn out good.

And that leads me to talk about an axis of thinking that we're calling the "future axis."[2] The future axis is the wrong axis because it's all about the future, what's going to be. The way Ricki and I talked about it is that both ends of that axis are the wrong place to be: "What's going to be if it's doom and gloom?" and even the other end, "What's going to be if everything turns out good?"

If that's where your mind is all the time, then you're always thinking about what's going to be—in the future.

---

2   Comment by Ely: The "future axis" is a term that Ricki and I coined to help us identify negative patterns in our own thoughts. In moments of weakness, we find ourselves on that axis.

None of that is good, because God runs the world. We don't know what's going to be, and we can't allow our worrying thoughts to just take us over and not allow us to live in the moment, not allow us to enjoy life. It results in anxiety. If our thoughts go to the doom-and-gloom side it results in depression. And even if our thoughts are on the good side (that all will turn out well), then if you get some news that causes a little doubt, then you automatically go to the other side of the axis again.

NOVEMBER 29, 2018/ 21 KISLEV 5779

Ely Medical Data

What's wrong with focusing on every symptom, the results of every test, every word that every doctor says? In essence, what's wrong with focusing on all the medical data?

For one thing, it defines the situation as beyond us—something technical characterized by test results, statistics, and potential side effects—and *not* as a human condition. That will cause everyone to relate to me *as a cancer, not as a person.*

More importantly, it is the wrong place for your thoughts to be. If you're constantly focusing on whether it's going to turn out good or whether it's going to turn out bad, you can't escape the worrying, the anxiety, the depression, and ultimately the despair. You're not able to think clearly, you're not able to fully integrate the information, your decision-making is going to be biased by fear. And if you're an onlooker or a caring family member or a friend, then all you're doing is thinking about "what if" and worrying. So it's just filled with uncertainty and fear and anxiety, and that's not helpful for anyone.

Additionally, the medical details are seemingly representative of reality, but in fact they're not. In fact, they're just bits of information and, oftentimes, just opinions of the experts.

Don't get me wrong—of course we have to do the tests, we have to collect the information, and we have to hear what the experts say. That's the best way we have for making decisions. But we must constantly remember that it's all partial information. It is only small samplings of the facts, as they are based on available diagnostic modalities. It does not predict what's going to be.

With the partial medical information, we start connecting the dots and we start predicting what's going to be: Am I likely to turn out healthy? Am I likely to turn out ill? Is this going to lead to a disastrous situation? And of course, our information and our ability to predict all that is very poor, and therefore, all the despair and anxiety and depression that comes along with that is unwarranted and it shouldn't be there. It is the wrong place to have our thoughts.

What determines what's going to be are many factors that we don't understand. And of course, we cannot forget that God's influence is pervasive and definitive, and we cannot understand its true nature. We cannot use our own logic to determine what's going to be. And we also cannot use just statistical information to know exactly what's going to be *in my case*.

My approach is to be relaxed, to go about my business, to enjoy life, and to enjoy relationships. Of course, we must undergo tests and collect opinions and make the best informed decisions, but we must remember that it's only the best we can do and it does not define what's going to be. It does not define the future.[3]

---

3   Comment by Ely at a later date: As I am writing these words while receiving chemotherapy at the oncology ward of Beilinson Hospital, it is hard to ignore the future axis. Relatively speaking, I am the healthy one here. Many old and sick people are in the various rooms, and occasionally, someone dies. There is a constant reminder of "sickness" and the seriousness of the condition that we call cancer.

Yet, I am trying to treat the medical aspects of this disease as merely technical details, and not allow them to invade my emotional being. Emotionally, I am upbeat, and even feel fortunate to be given the opportunity to confront a challenge like this. Facing this challenge is an opportunity for growth and a refinement of the search for meaning in my life. It has brought me closer with Ricki in a way that is unique to two people going through a challenge together. It has also forged stronger connections with many family and friends.

NOVEMBER 29, 2018/ 21 KISLEV 5779

Ricki Squamous Cell

"What is a squamous cell anyway?" Ely asked. Or rather, stated.

Those words made a big difference for me this morning. We have a tendency to think that cancer has a mind of its own. That it decides how and where to spread, whether to wreak havoc or whether it will disappear.

But in reality, the same God that created every biological entity, including every different type of cell, created the cancerous cells as well. And the same God that decides who will receive what challenge is the same God who decides whether a particular cancer will be cured or not. He is the same God who provided the circumstances for us to detect the disease at a particular stage. And He is the same God who decides how long a person should live in this world. We cannot possibly fathom His ways, just like we cannot possibly fathom the variety of cells and the complexity of these cells.

This gives me great comfort. The enormity of God's world is simply beyond our comprehension. But one thing we do know, both from Judaism and from experience, is that God is good. The ultimate Good. And that is a concept that we also cannot fully grasp. We can barely scratch the surface of this Good in our human experience. Ely and I are totally with Hashem's plan for us, knowing that we are in the best "hands," with or without an understanding of what that really means.

NOVEMBER 29, 2018/ 21 KISLEV 5779

Ely *Bitachon*

How am I able to maintain my attitude of positivity in this situation? The simple answer is total *bitachon* in Hashem—total trust in God. Confidence that God runs the show. It's His world run by His rules. We don't understand all those rules. We don't understand all the mechanisms. We don't understand the ultimate purpose. We do what we can. We do what we should do based on the wisdom and the understanding that we are granted. But ultimately, we don't have full knowledge and full understanding and full vision.

We, as human beings, are put on a path in life, and we have to try to follow that path. In order to do so, we must see where the path is. That path may twist and turn. We may think we know where it's heading, but in truth we really don't. Oftentimes, it twists one way and the other way and then we understand later that we thought we were heading in one direction, but it was much better for us to go in a different direction.

The point is that this is the way the world works. Everything is ultimately for the good. That is, actually, a fact—a fact similar to the facts of nature. You can plant a seed in the ground, water it, give it proper conditions of sunlight and so on, and watch it grow. That is an amazing fact. It involves many, many, many components that we don't understand. The very nature of life is what we don't understand. We have to maintain the perspective that, also, the events that happen in life are similar; they are under the direction of God, but the ultimate purpose is unknown. Whatever God decides is for the good because God is benevolent and cares for us. Just, we don't always understand what is good for us. We don't understand the definition of good. Sometimes what we think is a bad outcome turns out to be good—and vice-versa.

It's very similar to a small child and a parent, where the small child doesn't quite understand what is good for him. The parent may insist that the child do annoying things, such as brush his teeth, or even painful things, such as being stung with a needle to immunize him from future disease. In such situations, the child is "forced" to suffer for some unknown reason to him, and will likely resent the parent. Nonetheless, it is the parent who has the greater sense of the "good" associated with these experiences.

This is my situation—and this is my attitude. I do not think about what should be and what might be, and I do not try to force matters. I do what I have to do. I have to pursue the modern methods of maintaining health and to finding what's wrong and pursuing the treatments that are available. Still, I know full well that all we can do is make the best decisions. All we have available to us is the knowledge that's available—which is never perfect—and treatments that are available, which are also not perfect. But we do the best we can, and it is our obligation to do so. Similarly, every step along the way, we have to keep full trust, full *bitachon*. Without that trust, we are just floating in midair. That's a matter of understanding the facts of how the world works. This is God's world. He created it. He created the rules. Those rules pertain all the time; this is just another example.

The ultimate outcome is not determined by us. We have to just keep our eyes open. I have to maintain the clarity of mind to know what I must do at all times. Whatever the outcome is, it will reflect God's will. That is full *bitachon*.

Chapter 5

The First Round of Treatment

We were informed by the doctors that there was no indication that the cancer had spread beyond the neck. That was a relief. However, the tumor in the neck was already quite substantial in size, and the doctors were concerned that performing the surgery at the outset could cause permanent damage to some of the nerves in the neck which control arm movement. In order to avoid potential handicap, they recommended a somewhat unconventional treatment plan (for this type of tumor), which included a round of very strong chemotherapy prior to the surgery, in the hope that this treatment would shrink the tumor enough to make the surgery more successful and less damaging. This chemotherapy regimen would require a six-day stay in the hospital.

DECEMBER 3, 2018/ 25 KISLEV 5779

Ely First Day of Chanukah

A personal note on this day, December 3rd, which is the first day of Chanukah.

I have a malignant cancer in my body, and as far as the tests can show, it has not spread to the rest of my body. It's just in my neck. It started from my tongue and spread to my neck. It's rather aggressive in the neck, so it must be treated quickly, so that it doesn't cause damage. We are trusting in the doctors to minimize the damage relating to all the treatment.

As I'm talking to my friends and family and telling them about this, it is at the same time somewhat difficult—because I'm bringing shocking news to people I care about—and also very comforting—because everybody who I care about is expressing a deep sense of kinship and love and caring. That positive energy is very helpful. The desire to help, the desire to pray, and the desire to get to the other side of this and be healthy and then get together and continue life is incredibly encouraging and supportive.

My own approach is as follows: This is part of life as much as is anything else. I don't know how this happened, and I don't know what's going to be. When you think about it, it is not too different than the other things that "happen" to us in life—we don't usually know why they happened nor what the outcome will be. So, this happened to befall me. It's God's will. There's no other way of explaining it.

It's an extremely unlikely event. As far as I know, I don't have any risk factors that I could have focused on to prevent this. It is just seemingly random—but not random at all. This is God's will. I believe that it's here for a purpose. It's here to drive positive change. It's here to focus my life, but I cannot understand why I was stricken with this. It may be a form of Divine punishment for something that requires fixing in my life, but I am not privy to God's plan and cannot know any details in that regard. This does drive me to seek to improve; it is not hard to find areas of character or moral behavior in need of improvement.

More importantly, it puts a very, very fine focus on the importance of life and the importance of using every moment in a constructive manner to accomplish what I need to accomplish in this world and not to waste time. I should not continue doing things that I shouldn't be doing; rather I need to use my time to do things that I know I should be doing but I've been putting off.

We all do this. We all think, "We'll get to that when we're older, when we're retired." As far as I'm concerned, life has changed. That's not going to happen.

I am making recordings and writing down deep thoughts that I've had that have been bottled up inside of me and now need to come out. They need to be organized, and the good ones need to be shared with others.

We each have a mission. This is a large part of my mission, in addition of course to the obvious missions of raising children and educating and helping others, and so on. So that is what we're doing. We have to remain positive. We have to use every moment. We have to remain happy. The physical pain and suffering—that may be, and will likely be. It's something that could be temporary and should not be the focus of anyone's thoughts. That does not scare me. That, we will get over. The problem would be any lasting disability that would prevent me from doing my work. That's the difficulty, and there, I can't be scared either because this is all God's plan.

I am in God's hands. He has sent very important professional messengers in the form of the doctors who are taking caring of me, and I will trust them. I will not second guess them or question them. I will ask intelligent questions, as any patient should. But I know I've been delivered to the right hands, and Ricki and I will walk hand in hand together in this. This is just another episode in life. We will use this as a challenge, overcome it, take it as an opportunity for growth.

DECEMBER 3, 2018/ 25 KISLEV 5779

Ricki Punishment?

Today, Ely put out a recording which stated that he believes that what happened to him may be a punishment, and he is taking it seriously and examining his actions to see where he needs to do *teshuvah*.

This was met by confusion and deep concern by close family members that maybe he does not think he is a good person and is walking around with a negative feeling. This is absolutely not the case, and I explained in a post afterwards that he meant that he sees this as a wake-up call. That we all have things to improve, even the greatest *tzaddikim*, and that he is taking the opportunity to examine his weaknesses. Not from a negative place, but rather from a place of: How can I use this experience to improve myself?

I also think that there is a basic premise that we have when we think about reward and punishment in Hashem's world, and that this premise is faulty. We tend to think of a single axis, with all people in the world somewhere along the axis. There are evil people on one end, righteous people on another end, and everyone else somewhere in the middle.

If we think of it that way, then it seems like sometimes the good people get the raw end of the deal while the bad people get plenty of reward. But I think the whole premise is wrong. We are not all in one basket. Every person is his or her own world, and within the world of *that* person, Hashem gives what is right for that person. Not in comparison to anyone else. Only in comparison to him/herself.

So for example, if a *tzaddik* has a negative trait that seems minor to others, then for *that* person, there might need to be some *tikkun*, and that person may receive a "wake-up call" or "punishment" to get them to pay attention. At the same time, someone who is far removed from being a *tzaddik* will not receive a "wake-up call" for that particular weakness. It is not relevant for him. On an individual person's scale, compared only to oneself, a person may receive other events to help that person move forward in life. In addition, challenges are experienced differently by different people.

The main point is to pay attention. If we pay attention to the messages that we are being given, and we use them in the right way, in an *individualized* way, then these messages can be used to push us forward in life, to help us grow, and ultimately to help us get closer to a purer version of ourselves.

DECEMBER 5, 2018/ 27 KISLEV 5779

Ricki Third Day of Chanukah

As I was saying *Al Hanisim* this morning, I noticed that the whole paragraph talks about the military victory, until the end—where it says that the Maccabees came into the Beit Hamikdash, sanctified it, lit candles, and established Chanukah.

It occurred to me that we are not celebrating the physical survival of the Jews, but rather their *reason* for survival. We are thanking Hashem for saving the Jews—so that they can bring light into the world. Only for that reason was a holiday established.

Similarly, in our current situation, we pray for Ely's recovery. But it's not simply about his physical recovery, so that he can just be in this world for the sake of being in the world. Rather, we are praying that he can stay in this world so that he can continue to bring light to the world, to Am Yisrael, to his family. *Refuah sheleimah l'Eliyahu Shmuel ben Leah.*

DECEMBER 5, 2018/ 27 KISLEV 5779

Ely First Phase of Treatment

Yesterday, Ricki and I were called into the hospital for an explanation of what the first phase of our treatment is going to look like. The doctors feel that surgery on the neck, in addition to the tongue, but specifically the neck, is going to be a very difficult surgery. It must be done because there's a lot of tumor in the neck, but they're very concerned that it is already causing some danger to the local structures: the blood vessels, the nerves, the muscles. And, all of that can mean not only great disability, but potentially great harm if they don't get it all out or if they damage those structures during the surgery. To try to prevent the difficulty and the damage, they've decided to give me a course of chemotherapy prior to the surgery.

So, Ricki and I were called in yesterday for an explanation of the chemotherapy. Tomorrow morning, we're going to call the ward and we're going to be told when to come in. A course of chemotherapy will be given over six days. Three very strong drugs will be infused into my vein. Those three drugs destroy the cells in the body that are in the process of dividing.

The process of division of a cell means it's growing—it creates more cells. That's what happens with a malignant cancer. It's in the process of growing. So these chemotherapeutic agents are designed to kill the cells that are growing, so it should hopefully kill the tumor. The problem is that it's a very primitive approach. It's not a targeted approach only to the tumor; it's like bombing the whole area because you're interested in only one little spot.

What happens is the entire body gets inflicted by this medication and all the cells in the body that are in the process of dividing in a normal, healthy way are also affected and are also killed. Hair cells for example, are going to be killed so the hair may fall out.

The immune system is going to be affected. The blood cells—the white blood cells, the red blood cells—but particularly the white blood cells, which are in the process of dividing and growing and constantly developing new cells in response to foreign invaders in the body, will be affected. So, my ability to fight infection is going to be decreased. That is a big risk with this type of therapy. I'm going to have to be very careful during the course of the infusion and for probably around two weeks thereafter.

And there may be other side effects as well. I hope and pray that the side effects will be minor and that I will get past this period. After recovery from the chemotherapy, the doctors will decide about the timing of surgery.

That's what's happening right now. I'm a little apprehensive about the chemotherapy, but for sure I am very happy to have it because it will be a major step toward reducing the tumor. The greatest threat here is the tumor, not the treatment. The treatment may present some risk, but the benefit far outweighs it. If we can reduce the tumor, we can get the tumor out in a way that it will no longer cause a threat to my body.

So, this is very good. I'm very pleased with the doctors and the attention that I'm getting. They're pushing everything forward in a quick way. *B'ezrat Hashem*, the cancer will be eradicated, and I will get back to good health.

DECEMBER 6, 2018/ 28 KISLEV 5779

Ely Thank You

Today, I will be going into the hospital for the start of a course of chemotherapy.

I must say that what has been extraordinarily positive and helpful in this whole experience is the outpouring of love and support from my dear family, from my close friends, and from people whom I haven't seen in years but with whom I have close ties; those ties are there and are well and alive.

The power of the positivity and the positive support is unbelievable, whether it's expressed in good wishes, whether it's expressed in offers for help, whether it's expressed in the promise to have me in mind for the *tefillot*, it doesn't matter. All of it is very positive, all of it helps.

B'ezrat Hashem, I will get past this, and *b'ezrat Hashem*, we will all be closer and we will focus on the positive things in life. We will focus our energies on doing our work. All too often we're distracted by annoyances, and those things seem very minor in light of what's going on now.

I want to thank everybody. I want to thank my close family, and I want to thank my close friends. Thank you.

DECEMBER 6, 2018/ 28 KISLEV 5779

Ely   My Personal Note on the Fourth Day of Chanukah

This morning, I'm about to go into chemotherapy, and this marks the very beginning of a chain of very difficult therapies which hopefully will totally eradicate the tumor that's inside of me. This is a difficult time.

Until now, I have felt this growing lump in my neck and I've become increasingly aware of the damage that it's doing. It's impinging more and more on the structures of my neck, around my throat, and I'm feeling more pain. This thing is getting bigger. It's clear it has to go.

It's not just one lymph node. It's a bunch of little ones as well. It all has to go. Surgery is necessary. There is no question about it, and the sooner the better. So, despite the fact that these treatments are going to be very difficult, I am very, very happy that we're moving along, and I must say that the care and attention that I've been getting has been unbelievable. I don't think anyone anywhere in the world can expect quicker service, better treatment, or more caring. It is extremely helpful for my spirit, and it is a clear sign that all of these people are messengers to do that work—whether they know it or not—because they are doing it faithfully. Thank God.

I am going into this process happily. The view that I have of life right now is extremely clear and positive. That is, apart from the knowledge that I don't know what the outcome is going to be, and I don't know how long I have to live (just as everyone who's reading this also does not know how long they are going to live). But that's not the topic right now. I am now being told that the situation is curable, because it has not spread to the rest of the body, and we have the means to eradicate the tumor. So, I'm going into this bravely and with prayers that I'm going to come out of it with no side effects or minimal side effects, minimal damage, and minimal residual problems that would impair my ability to do my work in this world.

My work in this world consists of, first and foremost, raising my children and being there for my close family and close friends. My work in this world includes clinical work and contributing in any way that I can to the forwarding of caring for neurological illness and general mental well-being. My role in this world includes messaging and telling people about keeping positive in difficult times. This includes helping people focus on the important things and not to be caught up in trivialities or the limitations of their own thinking. Rather, to keep a broad perspective—to see the world for what it is, for the complexities and the beauty of what it is. To see people for who they are, and to appreciate the power behind it, the Supreme Being—Hashem, the God Who created the world. The God Who keeps the world going and determines events of the world. The God Who has a plan for us, Who is good and always, always has our well-being in mind as individuals and as people. The God Who will one day bring the *geulah* according to His will and His plan.

That's the reality in which I live. Knowing that reality, feeling that reality, and living that reality is very comforting. It brings joy and allows me to go happily through every step in life—whether it seems to be difficult, whether it seems to be painful, or whether it seems to be joyous. That is because nothing is chance or happenstance. Everything has a greater purpose even though we usually cannot understand it. So, we should be happy with what we do understand. We should be happy with those small glimpses into the truth of the natural world and the greater universe revealed by science. But we should be modest in keeping everything in perspective according to the very limited knowledge that we have and the very limited capabilities of our understanding and our overall perspective.

So let's understand and enjoy the goodness and the miracles and Chanukah. And let us pray that all of us, all my loved ones—enjoy life and look upon every single day of life as an opportunity to improve and to focus our energies on our true missions, and that we all be *zocheh* to warrant the teamwork and the love that we share between us and the love that we get from God and that ultimately, we are around to see the *geulah*. That is my prayer.

DECEMBER 6, 2018/ 28 KISLEV 5779

Ricki   Miracles of Chanukah

I am not sure what got me so emotional, and I'm not sure I can articulate it. But there was something so unbelievable about lighting Chanukah candles in the oncology ward of Beilinson hospital, with Ely hooked up to his first chemotherapy treatment, and all different types of people lighting together.

This is what it is like to be in the hospital in Eretz Yisrael on a *chag*, a Jewish holiday. Am Yisrael coming together, young and old, healthy and ill, Chassidic and Sephardic, all celebrating the miracles of Hashem in this world—in a place where people are praying for miracles. There is something very special about sharing that moment.

DECEMBER 8, 2018/ 30 KISLEV 5779

Ricki   Shabbat in the Oncology Ward

I will try to convey a little bit of what we experienced this Shabbat. Here we are, in the oncology ward of Beilinson hospital. We find ourselves here on Shabbat Chanukah, Rosh Chodesh. Our tendency might have been to stay to ourselves. After all, what do we have to do with other people that just happen to be here as well? Why interact?

However, we discovered that by reaching out, it really helped us as well.

Ely was starting to feel some side effects on Friday evening. Some hiccups, slight nausea, some tiredness. But when we started reaching out to people, all of that just disappeared.

It started with the candle lighting before Shabbat. There was a woman there who said, How can we be happy in a place like this?

Ely started talking to her, and let her know that there is a way to be happy, and there are people who can help. Her response to his kindness was palpable. From there, we went into Shabbat. As we davened in our room, a *dati* woman walked by, and asked us if she and her mother could please join us when we make Kiddush. So when we were ready for Kiddush, we went into their room. We sang *Shalom Aleichem*, and *Eishet Chayil*, and then Ely made Kiddush.[1] The daughter's name was Orly, and the mother was Esther. The mother looked very ill. She was lying in bed, and it was difficult for her to talk. Ely explained what kind of cancer he has, and he asked her what she has. She said that she has it everywhere. She said that she is twenty years older than him, and that her daughter is getting married in two weeks. They told us that they are Persian Jews, and they talked a bit about their family. We talked to her and to her daughter, and gave them some words of *chizuk* and comfort. The image of her lying there, with a scarf draped around her head, and the words coming out with great effort and obvious discomfort, will stay with me for a long time.

After that, we ate our soup, and then decided to go out and see who else might want to hear Kiddush. This was really Ely's initiative, and although I was very happy that we were reaching out to people, I didn't necessarily feel like continuing. But seeing what it did for Ely, and the look on his face as we were talking to people, propelled me forward. I realized that his well-being is highly dependent on doing things for others, as well as on my support of those efforts and perhaps my initiation of them too. The thought that going out into the ward would keep him feeling well immediately motivated me to keep going. So we did.

We went to one room, where we had met the patient and her daughter earlier. We offered to make Kiddush for them and they happily accepted. From there, we went to the nurses' station and asked if they knew of anyone else that might want to hear

---

1   Most of the people we met, whether from religious backgrounds or not, were familiar with the songs as well as the Kiddush.

Kiddush. The nurse on call was a little puzzled by our question, and thought that we were looking for *dati* people. When we explained to her that we were thinking of all Jews, a woman came by and the nurse asked her if she wanted to hear Kiddush. She said yes, and we happily accompanied her to her room. She was the mother of a forty-five-year-old man, Shalom, who was the patient. Shalom explained that he has been fighting various forms of cancer since the age of twenty-seven. He was watching TV, but put the TV on silent while we were there. His mother gave him a napkin to put on his head, and we sang *Shalom Aleichem* and made Kiddush. We talked to them a bit and then left.

After that, we checked in with Moshe, our eighty-seven-year-old neighbor/roommate from the day before, who also happened to be a lawyer still in active practice and running his own office. He was not available, so we returned to our meal. After eating, we checked in with him again, and he was happy to hear Kiddush. He had family members there, including teenage grandchildren, and the experience that we had in that room was quite profound. As we sang, Moshe joined in, with a look of pure joy and ecstasy on his face. His children and grandchildren looked on, apparently never having seen this side of him before. He later explained to us that he used to know all the words but he had forgotten some of them. This experience seemed to lift his spirits, and we left with a very good feeling.

Wow.

What a powerful experience. Here is Ely, hooked up to an IV, walking around the ward together with me, making Kiddush and giving *chizuk* to many other people. We are sure that the people benefitted from this, but what it did for Ely was incredible to watch. His (relatively mild) symptoms just disappeared. He was feeling good, strong, and full of energy and purpose.

On Shabbat morning, we davened in the room again. When we got to what would normally be the reading of the Torah portion,

Ely got ready to read from a *Chumash*.[2] But we decided to see if Orly and her mother wanted to join in. We stopped by their room, and Esther was resting but Orly came with us to the family area, and we sat there and he read the Torah portion. Shalom's mother joined us at some point as well. This too was a remarkable experience, and as I watched Ely's face, I saw that he was actually glowing.

The rest of Shabbat was spent resting, eating, talking, and singing. As we were singing during *seudah shlishit*, we decide to go see if anyone was around and wanted to talk or even sing. We found Moshe in the family area, and we talked to him for some time. Then when it was time, we davened *Maariv* and then came out for *Havdalah* and candle lighting. Once again, Moshe was moved, and insisted on setting up an additional *chanukiyah* so that he could make the *berachot* on his own. Orly commented on Ely's voice, and how thankful she was that we were part of her Shabbat. Later, as we were eating dinner, Shalom's mother passed by and asked if we had already made *Havdalah*. That was a surprise! So we told her that we had, but that we would do it again. Shortly after that, we congregated again in the lighting area, and we made *Havdalah*. Shalom also made the *berachot* on the Chanukah candles, and we sang.

A very inspiring Shabbat—in the oncology ward.

DECEMBER 11, 2018/ 3 TEVET 5779

Ricki Last Day, Round I

Here we are, the last day of treatment for this round of chemo-therapy. It's been a long week. It's hard to see Ely feeling weak and sick. That is so not him.

---

2   Ely was a *ba'al koreh*, a person who regularly reads from the Torah. The circumstances we found ourselves in did not allow for him to read from an actual Torah scroll, so instead he read from a book, without the blessings.

Chapter 6

Recovery from Chemotherapy

At the end of the very intense chemotherapy regimen that Ely received, we were told that the recovery would take another ten days or so, and that the first five would be the worst. We were told to expect fatigue, flu-like symptoms, lack of appetite, and possibly other side effects as well. We were sent home to recover.

It is difficult to describe why the recovery was so difficult, and what Ely was feeling during this time. I guess the best way to describe it is like the worst flu you have ever had, times ten. But we were told not to give in to the fatigue—to try to get out for walks every day, and to try to eat and drink as much as possible.

DECEMBER 12, 2018/ 4 TEVET 5779

Ely After Chemotherapy

I returned from the hospital last night, where I received six days of a very intensive chemotherapy—quite an experience. In the beginning, it wasn't bad. I was feeling okay, but then toward the end, I had very, very uncomfortable feelings of fatigue, and I couldn't eat anything. It was terrible.

This morning, I'm feeling a lot better, thank God. They say that the next week to ten days are going to be very difficult.

B'ezrat Hashem, we'll get through it, and then we'll move to the next phase.

I'm sitting out on the balcony now. It's dark. I'm looking up at the clouds and the stars. It's a wonderful feeling. The clouds and the stars are the creations of God. These remind me of the constant grounding that I must have, and my life here as a functionary to do whatever God wants me to do. But the world goes on with the mission and the plan that God has for it.

The most important thing to remember always is that we as humans are weak in our thinking. We don't understand everything. We cannot understand everything. It's not possible. We can be happy with what we understand. We can be joyous when we feel the emotions of being close to the truth and being close to God, but if we can get used to the idea that we don't understand everything, then we can be happy with ourselves and what happens to us in life.

DECEMBER 12, 2018/ 4 TEVET 5779

Ely A Message to My Family and Friends: I Am Not My Cancer

I am not my cancer. The cancer is just a foreign invader that has to be eradicated, and it's causing trouble in my body, and the treatment is also causing trouble in my body—but those are temporary, minor nuisances. They do not define me, so please treat me as a person, not as a bunch of symptoms.

I know everyone is concerned and they want to know all the details. What's going to be? How do I feel? Do I have this symptom? Do I have that symptom?

That kind of talk brings me into the realm of being sick. It's not good for me, and I prefer to talk about being healthy.

So please—I know it's hard because everyone is curious, but I'll try to keep everyone updated on the technical details. When communicating with me, please keep it on the human level, about us, about people, about living, about being healthy and continuing and thriving, and not about everything that's going wrong and the difficulties.

Thank you.

DECEMBER 13, 2018/ 5 TEVET 5779

Ricki Things Don't "Just Happen"

I saw a video yesterday about a young woman who grew up with very strong Christian faith, and has been diagnosed with terminal cancer. She essentially has come to the conclusion that sometimes things "just happen." While she negates the notion of direct reward and punishment, it seems from the interview that she would rather believe that life is random rather than God is cruel. Given those limited possibilities, her choice is understandable.

But why are those the only two choices? Is it not possible that life is *not* random, that things happen for a reason, and that God is *good*? Why do we think that we need to understand the system?

If you believe that God created the world, do you not also believe that He created death? Why? Isn't that cruel? Well, maybe it's not cruel, and maybe we just don't understand the real meaning behind it. Similarly, why someone has to die at a certain age or in a certain way can be (and I believe is) fully directed, but not understandable to us.

I have been trying to understand why some people find it comforting to believe that things "just happen." Somehow, the notion of randomness is more palatable than the idea that God is behind all events in the world. But first of all, this is not the reality. God is all-powerful, and it is by His will that the earth exists every second. So too, it is by His will that certain people are faced with certain events in their lives. If you stop and think about things that have happened to you, you can sometimes see the wisdom behind those things. But sometimes, we can't see the wisdom at all.

Does that mean there is no wisdom? That it is just a roll of the dice? I think it requires a healthy dose of humility, *anavah*, to realize that although there are things that we can understand and figure out, those things are but a small proportion of what we cannot understand and cannot figure out. Do we understand even the basic mechanisms of how a person is created? How the brain and thinking and consciousness happen? How seeds grow and animals reproduce?

Why do we think we can understand why—and how— events happen?

I truly believe that every event that happens to us in our lives is specific and directed from Above. I also believe that there is reward and punishment, but that the mechanism for that is way more complex than we can ever understand.

In order to put the young woman's suffering into proportion, first we have to understand a basic truth: Everyone dies. The same good God that created life also created death. The question of why she might have to die young is a different question than why she has to die, but we tend to ask the latter rather than the former. Who knows the answer to that question? Who knows if it has to do with her specific role in the world, or with generations to come, or any other reason? We do not know the reason, but I am quite sure there is a reason. But it is a Reason with a capital "R". And it is not for us to figure out the reason.

If we believe that God is all-powerful and that God is Good, we can relax. We can rely on His goodness.

DECEMBER 14, 2018/ 6 TEVET 5779

 Grounding My Thoughts

How to ground my thoughts. It is now three days, the third day since my discharge from the hospital for chemo. I'm still very weak, and I'm still feeling very bad. I'm sitting out here on my balcony before sunrise and I came to this understanding that my thoughts are not grounded. That was very disconcerting. I am thinking about my suffering and my troubles, and my thoughts are just running around in my head and I cannot latch onto a good thought. My head just keeps going to annoying thoughts and to a vague hope that this is going to end soon. But my secret to thriving is not that. It is to find the grounding, to find that thought that will allow me to escape the thoughts of suffering and will allow me to even feel good and be productive in this state. That's why I come out here to the balcony; because sitting out here in the cold fresh air, looking up at the stars in the dark sky—is comforting. This, to me, is one of the constants in the world, the nature that God created—that has been this way for a long time and will not change, as far as we know.

This helps, but it's not enough. Just the realization that I need grounding is already pretty good. Otherwise, I am just wrapped up in my own misery. That grounding thought can be many different things for different people, but for me it is a focus on my overall mission, on my partner in life, on my position here in the world, which hasn't changed one iota.

DECEMBER 17, 2018/ 9 TEVET 5779

Ricki Grasping at Comfort Straws

We all do it. Let's start with the easiest and most pronounced example nowadays. Smartphones. How many times per hour do you check yours? Do you find it difficult to leave it on the side for a period of time? Why is that? Somehow, there is something comforting about checking to see if anyone has pinged, or checking the news or our emails. But the comfort is short-lived, and actually leads to a need to have more of it. Sort of like chocolate, but that's a topic for a different chapter. The whole entertainment industry is based on this need that we have. In that case, it is accomplished by providing a distraction. Or a story which is more troubling than whatever it is we are dealing with in life. In short, it is a fantasy.

I am going to argue that there is another form of this, which is just as frequent and just as unsatisfying in the end. This became clear to me as we were finishing the first round of treatment and gearing up for what was still to come. Today is our first appointment with the oncologist since the chemotherapy treatment started ten days ago. I don't know if we will have any more information or if we will have to wait a bit longer to hear what the rest of the plan is. But I do know that the very fact that we have this appointment got me onto the "information seeking" track. I was led here by a combination of factors, including the fact that I had time to myself at night (a recipe for getting sucked into places you shouldn't go, including comfort food), it was a stressful time period, and my sister had just informed me of the positive outcome for actor Michael Douglas, who apparently suffered from the "same thing" and survived and is thriving. So I found myself looking at websites about oral cancer, or about the surgery that Ely is likely to undergo, or about the therapy options (and potential side effects) post-surgery. Why did I feel the need to do this?

Somehow, I thought it would give me comfort. There's something comforting about surfing the Internet, looking for information. But in reality, it is only a distraction. It doesn't offer any real comfort at all.

Chapter 7

What's Next?

Our meeting with the oncologist resulted in an unexpected conclusion. Dr. Kursitz insisted that since there was no clear response with the first round of chemotherapy, a second round would have to be done prior to attempting the surgery. She said that a minimum of two rounds was required in order to attempt to shrink the tumor. We had thought that the plan was for one round and then surgery, so we were quite surprised by this conclusion. And somewhat dismayed. But we quickly collected ourselves and geared up for the next phase of this journey. We now had about ten more days of recovery ahead of us, and then it would be time for the next hit.

DECEMBER 18, 2018/ 10 TEVET 5779 (MINOR FAST DAY)

Ely This Is a Purposeful Turn in My Life

At first, I didn't know what to think about the situation. When I started to think that I would be cured or totally treated because the doctor said so, it was tempting to think, "Let's get past it quickly. Let's get back to regular life, back to what I was doing before. This episode is just a nuisance and we'll put it behind us."

Now, I see it differently. I don't know what my outcome is going to be, of course. I don't know that it's going to be bad, good, or in-between. But what's clear to me is that this episode in my life is very purposeful. It's here for a reason. And I believe the main reason is to carry forward a certain change in myself, in my outlook, and in my activities. Things are not going to go back to what they were.

My activities during this period, while I'm sick and while I'm undergoing treatment, are actually going to be meaningful and productive, just in a very different way than they were before.

This is not just a statement of hope. I'm actually seeing this. The type of productivity that I'm seeing is a different type of thought, a different type of insight, and as a result, I'm able to understand different things and communicate those things to others.

DECEMBER 18, 2018/ 10 TEVET 5779

Ely On Slowing Down

One of the things that I've been forced to do since I've started the chemo is simply to slow down.

It's true. Even before the chemotherapy, since I was first aware that there was a cancer in my body, it caused my whole being to slow down and think and appreciate and consider every moment and every decision in a different way than before. But that's different than what's going on now. Now I am physically weak. I have no choice: I have to walk slowly. I have to speak slowly. I have to eat slowly. I have to pray slowly. When Ricki and I walk outside, we walk slowly, step by step. We look at the trees. We look at the grass. We notice the sky. We notice people. We have a different sense of appreciation for the world around us. Ricki has mentioned a number of times that this has forced her to slow down, and that's been a good thing. It's a totally different appreciation of the world.

The greatest difference for me is in my prayer. When I pray every morning, afternoon, and evening, each prayer has a set format. Practically my entire life I've been saying the Jewish prayers; I know it by heart and know it well.

That's a problem because what happens when you know it well is that you don't need to pay attention to the words. Often, I tend to go into auto-pilot and say it without really understanding that I even said it, or perhaps if I did, without knowing what the words meant to me at that moment. When I go to *shul*, the pace is so fast that it is literally impossible to spend time on every word.

What I'm doing now while I'm davening at home is I'm just going slowly at my own pace, but I'm saying it word by word. I don't physically have the strength to say every single paragraph, every single prayer, every single *Tehillim*, but I am saying different ones at different times, and each one takes on a meaning that it never had. This is because I'm slow, I'm deliberate, I'm concentrating, and of course, my davening takes a long time. This is a good thing that's changing my life. Right now, I'm forced to do it. I expect that this is going to carry forward—maybe not to this degree—but it must.

DECEMBER 18, 2018/ 10 TEVET 5779

Ricki   No Expectations

No expectations. That's the lesson for today. Not for good and not for bad. This whole notion of "what to expect" is not right.

It pops up in many different ways. Here are some examples:

- I spoke with a woman who was familiar with the type of cancer Ely has. She told me a little bit about "what to expect" from the surgery. I realized after that conversation that although it might be comforting to hear of an ultimately good outcome, it was not helpful to hear about what to expect, since (a) her story is still different than Ely's, no matter what; and (b) some of her actual experiences were pretty lousy and I'm not ready to hear those things just yet. Most people feel the need to know. But then, that sets up **expectations**, which either causes fear or hope but inevitably puts us on the "future axis."

- We had thought that Ely was receiving one course of chemotherapy, followed by surgery and then additional treatments. We found out on Monday that he will need an additional course of chemotherapy before the surgery. This caused us to pause, take a moment to equilibrate, and then go on. When other people asked if this was expected or not, we realized that there should be absolutely no expectations. Not for good and not for bad—because in fact, we don't even know what that means. We have no way of assessing what is good and what is bad. We can just rely on our *shlichim*, our messengers, to lead us in the right way, step by step.

DECEMBER 19, 2018/ 11 TEVET 5779

Ely How Am I Feeling Today?

Today is the eighth day after my course of chemotherapy. I can say that I actually feel like myself today. Yesterday, I felt much better than the day before, and each day, I've been feeling stronger and stronger. Each day, I look back and I think, "Oh my God, I must have been feeling really bad if this is how I feel now." It's an amazing thing.

As I experience things, I get better day by day. But when I look back, I realize that I was really doing poorly. I was knocked out, and I was really tired. I was suffering from terrible feelings of not being able to eat and pains in my stomach. But I also realize that I shouldn't look back. I have to live in the moment. If I live in the memory of what must have been, it only makes things worse. And it makes it scarier for the next time.

I feel great that I can say that I started to feel like myself. I don't actually feel fully like myself. I'm already thinking in my head, "Okay, maybe it's time to start exercising again," but that's ridiculous. I don't have the strength to exercise. I barely have the strength to get out of bed and get dressed and think about what

I'm going to be doing today. My brain, though, is much more active. My brain is able to complete thoughts that I couldn't complete a few days ago. True, I cannot think the way I normally would, but I'm still thankful for this state, because I feel much better. Every day that I feel better, I feel good, I feel thankful. I'm now looking forward to what I'm going to do today.

So the answer to "How am I feeling?" is "I'm feeling good." It doesn't mean I'm back to myself because I'm sure I don't have all the capabilities that I had in the past. I'm going to have to rest a few times today. I have to go slowly; I'll have to have very limited activities.

But still, I'm feeling good. Today is my anniversary with Ricki, and I intend to have a great day.

DECEMBER 19, 2018/ 11 TEVET 5779

Ely   In Between Chemotherapies

We are now firmly past the first chemo, and in about one week, I'm going to be starting the next chemo.

I must say that this has been a progressive journey. I have been feeling closer and closer to God, and closer and closer to Ricki, and closer and closer to my loved ones. My friends and my community have been incredible. The doctors, the nurses, and the caring people who are doing their jobs have been incredible. Is it just that they have been superlative, or is it my subjective appreciation of them?

There is no question that my appreciation of living in the world and for the incredible beauty of the world has been sharpened since I first found out that I might have a problem. But, it's been getting much, much sharper.

I believe that I am going to come out of this stronger, healthier, with a better outlook on life, and a better focus on what I'm supposed to be doing every day and every hour. I believe that I'm going to come out of this with a much greater sense of what true *chessed* is and how to deliver it. This is an area in which I feel I was deficient earlier in my life. I believe that every step along the way is purposeful—that every treatment along the way, and every difficulty along the way, as well as every joy along the way is meaningful and purposeful and is there to build character for myself and Ricki, and for all those around us who are also involved in our journey.

And the only thing that can come out of this if we do it better is that we will have clearer understanding of what our mission is here in the world—what our role is, how to do it, and how to communicate its message. And *b'ezrat Hashem*, when we're fully able, we will go out and do it.

That very positive outlook is a real belief. It doesn't contradict the idea that anything that Hashem wants will happen. If that is not Hashem's will, so be it.

And I shall be as happy with that as with a more "positive outcome"—and so should everyone else. But from what I'm seeing, there's so much positivity in this that it's a promise for the future. It's a promise and it's an obligation on my part.

DECEMBER 19, 2018/ 11 TEVET 5779

Ely Living without a Sense of Taste

I want to talk about the incredible importance and wonder of having a taste for food. I now appreciate that a taste for food is quite complex. When I can't eat, it isn't just a lack of appetite or having to be reminded. It is also an aversion to most foods, and the different foods involved change over time so that each time I need to eat, it is a chore to figure out what I can manage.

It becomes almost tortuous to eat. It takes a lot of effort, it takes a lot of planning to think, "Okay. What would taste reasonable to me right now?" By reasonable, I don't mean enjoyable.

So, what I'm experiencing about food is an incredible appreciation for how God created the world with foods that are tasty to people and with people's brains that are designed to appreciate those foods. There's a match. It's amazing. It should be appreciated. I know that before I had my illness, I didn't appreciate it. I might have given it lip service here and there, but I didn't appreciate it this way.

At this moment, I've not appreciated the taste of any kind of food in over a week. It seems like a lifetime. It's probably going to continue for another few weeks, as long as this chemotherapy is continuing. It may even continue longer. I'm not sure. No matter what, the important thing for me to understand now is how important taste is. Taste and smell are examples of goodness "built in" to nature. We need to thank God for the wonders of the world and how He designed it so that it's good for people. Thank You.

DECEMBER 19, 2018/ 11 TEVET 5779

Ricki   Eighth Anniversary

Today is our eighth anniversary.

Last night, I went to sleep early. Really early. Before 9 p.m. I woke up at 12:30 and felt wide awake. So I left the bedroom and read for about an hour or so. When I felt I could go back to sleep, I got up and started walking back toward the bedroom. Suddenly, out of nowhere, I was hit with a wave of: "Is this really happening? Can it be true that Ely has CANCER? Do we really have to go through this?" and I started to cry. I didn't let it go too far—I immediately reminded myself that yes, this is the reality, and that it is happening for a reason. I reminded myself not to get onto the future axis (worry versus hope). I said a little prayer and I went back to bed.

But still, it was hard to fall asleep. There was a heaviness that I felt. Despite all of the positive thinking that we have been doing, this is obviously a process and does not always follow a straight path. Part of the difficulty is accepting the huge change in our daily lives. It almost seems as if things will never be "normal" again. But of course, things are not supposed to be "normal," and that is actually one of the blessings of this situation. I called the folder in my computer for my journal entries "Our New Life," and I really mean that in a positive way. The adjustment does take time, though.

So on this day, on our anniversary, I want to take a few moments to express some things that I am thankful for:

- I am thankful for the clarity and insight that we have been given.
- I am thankful for the love between us.
- I am thankful for the wonderful caregivers—from the doctors to the nurses to the cleaning help on the ward. Really, each one is caring and warm and it helps tremendously.
- I am thankful for our strong family, who loves and cares and asks about our well-being and is always willing to do whatever they can.
- I am thankful for the circle of support that we have found—from friends to acquaintances, from work colleagues to *Rabbanim*, from extended family members to people who I don't even know.
- I am thankful for the beautiful days we have been given during this recovery time, which have allowed us to take walks every day.
- I am thankful for the flexible work schedule that Hashem has given me, which always seems to be heavier at times when I can work more and lighter at times that I cannot. The *hashgachah* in that fact alone is remarkable.
- I am thankful for all of our children, who are finding their individual paths in life one by one. I am thankful for the fact that Hashem is taking care of each and every one of them, protecting them in ways that I cannot.
- I am thankful for the ability to express myself.
- I am thankful for Ely's guidance and wisdom, and his total *mesirut nefesh*.

- I am thankful for the *chessed* that Hashem has given us in the ability to enjoy our food.
- I am thankful for the opportunity to live each day.

DECEMBER 19, 2018/ 11 TEVET 5779

Ricki The Beauty That Is Everywhere

We went out for our daily walk, and at first, I knew there was still a baseline level of tension that seemed to be present all the time. We sat down on a bench and started to actively relax. I had this realization that I am like a vessel: when I am filled with tension, worry, fear, there is no room for the goodness to enter. I realized that I had to clean out the negative feelings to make room for the positive. So I started to concentrate on that. Suddenly, I was able to appreciate so much that was right there in front of my eyes. The beautiful trees, each one with its own shape and color, the bright blue sky with the slowly moving clouds over a tall building, the presence of Ely, sitting right there next to me, the cool breeze and the soft sounds around us. A moment later, I noticed some dark purple flowers that I hadn't noticed just a second earlier. And I realized that the more you look, the more you see. Beauty unfolds before your eyes.

We continued walking, and I started to notice all the various plants and trees on the way. "Who ever notices these things?" I asked. Often, we feel the need to get away—to see different scenery—and at those times, we appreciate the beauty around us. When we have traveled to the Dead Sea, for example, we've been struck by the beauty of the desert brown against the blue sky. But rarely, if ever, do we appreciate the beauty in our own backyard. This reminded me of something Tamar (our daughter) said to me this morning as we were leaving the house. She noticed a particularly beautiful flowering plant at the entrance to our building. She stopped to look at it, and she said, "Wow, I can't believe we have this in our very own garden."

That is a sentiment that we all ought to cultivate.

Ely Focus

Each day, I've been feeling stronger and stronger. Each day, I've been spending more time awake and not sleeping. I've been eating better. What's amazing is, as good as I feel, I'm very acutely aware of how I'm nowhere near my normal level of functioning. Thoughts sometimes pop into my head of taking care of some business affairs or starting to exercise or doing things at the pace that I normally would, and I quickly realize how ridiculous those thoughts are. I've settled into the idea that my work now during this period of time—which is likely to last the next few months—is just to concentrate on being healthy, taking care of myself, and most importantly, being with Ricki and developing ourselves and nurturing our thoughts together. At this time, without the worries of work, I'm more free to allow myself to think about the higher things in life, the more spiritual matters—the connection with God. When I spend time in my prayers these days, it's much more meaningful. Everything is slower, I say things word by word, whether it's *Birkat Hamazon* or *tefillot*, I actually pay attention to what I'm saying, I mean what I'm saying, and it has an effect on me. And that lifts me even higher.

So what's been happening over this past time, and I pray that it continues, is that I have better and better focus and better and better *kavanah* and have higher and higher feelings and thoughts. That's what's happening now.

What all this is doing is it's lifting me to a place that is very positive, and it is taking less and less effort to maintain a true positive outlook on my situation. It's a true gift and a blessing. Any physical suffering that happens, I am able to deal with on the way toward this spiritual uplifting. I am experiencing a cleansing of character, a refreshing of my life, a review of the meaning of the use of my time and energy, and new understanding of my particular gifts and abilities.

All of that is truly a gift, which when we're in the usual run of life, we don't have the bandwidth to think about. We just keep going, and sometimes we can change or improve in minor, incremental ways. But what's happening now is a quantum change.

Thank you, Hashem. I have incredible appreciation for my life with Ricki. I have incredible appreciation for my wonderful support, including and first of all my parents, my brother, my sister-in-law, all my children, and the incredible friends and many acquaintances and strong people in my life. All of that is coming to light, all of that is special and meaningful and very positive, and all of that feeds back so I can be positive and then share with others. Have a good day.

DECEMBER 23, 2018/ 15 TEVET 5779

Ely *Dayeinu*

This is a note for all the wonderful people who are now expressing support and encouragement and prayer—my wonderful family, friends, and community.

I'm sitting here out on the balcony, before sunrise. There's a big, full, bright moon out in the sky. It is beautiful. There are some fluffy clouds I can see. There are some stars. It's just wonderful to be here.

Yesterday, Ricki and I had a mini celebration for a "*dayeinu* moment." We paused and thanked God for my feeling good. Let's call it a recovery after the first round of chemotherapy.

This is a victory. I'm pretty much feeling back to myself. And we've delivered a major blow to the cancer. Possibly even a lethal blow. We don't know. The fact that the mass is still large in my neck doesn't necessarily mean that there are live cancer cells in there—so we were told by our oncologist.

So, this is a pretty big moment. It doesn't mean we're done. It means there was a major step. I had a major victory. Now, we're going to prepare ourselves for the next round of chemotherapy.

The doctors have decided to hit the cancer even harder with another round. And so on with every step. We're going to pause, and we're going to thank God. This is like the song we sing during the Pesach Seder, *Dayeinu*. In the Passover story, there were many steps that are listed in the *Dayeinu* song.

Still, something in the song does not make sense. Would it really have been enough (the literal meaning of "*dayeinu*") for God to have taken us out of Egypt and not given us the Torah at Mount Sinai? The text says that, but how does it make sense? Isn't it clear to us now, after the fact, that there was an end game of God carrying us through all the various steps in order for us to reach the Promised Land of Israel and to set up a nation in that land? Indeed, it seems that we should not be satisfied with anything less than the complete process that started with the exodus from Egypt and culminated with the building of the Beit Hamikdash in Jerusalem!

However, this is not the way it works as you are going through life. From your perspective "in the moment," each miracle along the way, each step toward redemption, and each revelation of God's helping hand are "*dayeinu* moments." They are moments when you pause in awe and gratitude while expressing appreciation for the goodness that you just received—understanding well that this step may be significant in the chain of events. You never know the ultimate outcome, but you can appreciate that an important step just occurred.

This is how I feel with regard to my illness. With every step, I'm getting healthier. And with every step, I'm coming closer to total eradication of the enemy, the cancer. I feel good and I need to express gratitude for every step along the way.

So let's go from small victory to small victory, like we always do when we go about our lives. There is no end; there is no complete victory. We have to keep moving, step by step. And that's what we're doing here, as well. So let's go on. I want to thank you for all the support that you're giving. It's wonderful and it is very helpful. It's keeping us on the positive side. We will keep on going and we will succeed.

DECEMBER 26, 2018/ 18 TEVET 5779

Ricki The Beauty of Variety in the World

I am truly amazed at the variety in the world. One aspect of this that I often talk about is the variety in individual humans. How can it be that there are billions of people in the world, and many multiple times that number of humans that have existed in the world until now, and that each one is different?!

If I try to draw a picture of a human, at best, I may come up with two or three variations (and they all will strangely resemble one form or another of a stick figure). Granted, I am no artist, but take people who are truly talented in art, and see how many variations they can come up with on their own. Hundreds? Maybe, but doubtful. Thousands? Almost unthinkable. Millions? No way. And yet, here we have a world with *billions* of people, each one different than the next. And not just different in looks—also different in personality, emotional makeup, physical and cognitive abilities, and many, many more aspects. This totally blows my mind. There is an infinite quality to it, which in my mind translates to the handiwork of God.

A different aspect of this is the number of species and sub-species in the animal world. I am fascinated by the fact that there are so many types of animals. I mean, just think about the animals that we are familiar with.

Let's take a zebra, for example. Who thought of putting black and white stripes on it? Or of putting eight legs on an octopus? Today we were out for a walk and we spotted a woodpecker. Wow. I was fascinated by the long pointy beak and the crown of feathers on its head, not to mention its unique colors. And that is just one type of bird, which is just one type of animal. When you start to think about it, it is truly mind-numbing.

I think that the most imaginative person in the world, if asked to come up with as many variations of living beings as possible, could never even come close to the number of variations that we find in the real world for just *one* type of animal. Take dogs. Or insects. Or birds. Each one of these has hundreds or thousands of varieties. And we haven't even discovered all of the types of animals. Every once in a while, you hear a report about a newly discovered species. This to me is another example of the vast greatness of God's world. And there is a beauty to it that is just unparalleled.

Of course, the same is true of plants and trees and flowers. Tall and short, an endless number of colors and shades of color, shady and pointy, those that change colors in the fall (or winter here in Israel) and those that don't, the list goes on and on. Literally you have to stop and smell the roses to garner an appreciation for all that is around us. The same is true for the fruits and vegetables that we eat. Who thought of a long, skinny, somewhat bent yellow fruit with a banana flavor? Or small little berries of various colors? What about an avocado or a mango? Each one has its unique shape, color, flavor and texture, and the varieties are mind-boggling.

It is not even necessary to go traveling around the world to find this beauty. We have discovered that just in our own neighborhood, there is so much variety and beauty in the animal and plant world, that just beginning to appreciate what is around us is a whole effort. But when we are calm and relaxed and in a good state, we really can appreciate it. And I have found that this appreciation also puts me into a more calm and relaxed state. It is a sort of positive feedback loop, where a certain level of calm and relaxation is required to get into the mode, but the more you see and appreciate, the more calm and relaxed you feel.

When you stop to appreciate these things, when you slow down enough to pay attention, it results in a good feeling. This is one of the ways that I have been dealing with this stressful situation. The blessing in our stressful situation is that it has forced us to slow down. To take long walks. To feel the sun on our face and watch the clouds. And to appreciate the unbelievable world that we live in and that God created just for us.

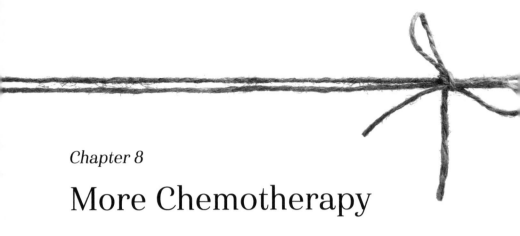

Chapter 8

More Chemotherapy

It was time to start again. Just a word about our family and friends during this time: Ely's parents were consistently available to help with Tamar (our only young child), but other than relying on them, we were initially in the mindset of doing this ourselves. Ely preferred not to have visitors in the hospital—even close family members (although some came anyway, and it's good that they did). We only minimally relied on friends, and that only when absolutely necessary.

Over time, though, we realized that this was the wrong approach. We needed to include close family and friends in many ways. We needed to allow them in: have them help, visit, and keep them regularly updated. It was not easy to do this—both because of privacy considerations and not wanting to impose on others. But after some time, we realized that it was really important to let other people help us. Our *rav* solidified this point for us, and he explained that it is actually a *chessed* to let people do *chessed* for you at times like this. This really changed our outlook, and ultimately helped us get closer to the people in our lives.

DECEMBER 27, 2018/ 19 TEVET 5779

Ricki Giving

Today we are starting the second round of chemotherapy. We had to leave the house at around 6:30 a.m., so we dropped Tamar off at the neighbor's house and off we went. In the car, I started imagining inviting all the supportive mothers/families to a *kiddush* that we want to make at the *shul* when we can. I imagined myself thanking them for their tremendous support and kindness. And then I pictured someone listening and thinking, "All I did was X (substitute some seemingly small act), while the other people here probably made major contributions." And while I was imagining this thought process, I realized that from *my* perspective, even a seemingly small thing—like picking Tamar up from school just one time, for example—was a *huge* contribution, because at that moment, it was exactly what I needed for peace of mind. I need to convey that message. The thanks and appreciation that I feel toward each and every person that has helped in any way is not dependent on the "size" of the task that they might have done. If it relieved me of a particular burden at a particular moment, then it was a tremendous help. This is true *chessed*. Helping someone with what they actually need, at the time that they need it. We often put our own ideas into what we think we can do for people, and we often berate ourselves for not doing enough, or worse, compare ourselves to others who seem to be doing more. What I am learning from this is that when I am in a position to give, I need to give what I can and what is suitable for me, and I do not need to think about what others might be giving. I need to be attuned to the needs of the receiving person, and make sure that it is the right thing, no matter how small it may seem to me.

DECEMBER 28, 2018/ 20 TEVET 5779

Ely Preparing

Yesterday we went into the oncology ambulatory treatment center for a treatment of chemotherapy, and today we're supposed to go in the morning to be hospitalized for five more days of continued treatment with other medications. The medications are the same as for the last chemotherapy treatment.

This time I feel I'm much better prepared, mentally and physically. I understand that even though overall it went well last time, I came back home feeling sick. I think it's not just because of the medication, but because of the environment. It's a hospital with very sick people...people who have cancer, people who are in and out of the hospital. Also, I had restrictions, including a limited variety of food that after a short time, I found repulsive. Having an IV in my arm and having to drag a pole around only allowed me to go up and down the hallway. I did practically no other exercise the whole time, and it was difficult.

Overall, those factors played an important role in my state of mind. This time I intend to do it differently.

- First of all, it's only five days instead of six days in the hospital, and that's good.[1]
- Second of all, I've been through it once before, and I know what to expect. Of course, that doesn't mean that I know everything that's going to happen, especially since the effects of the treatment are supposed to be cumulative. So, it could be that some of the side effects might be more severe than before, and there may be side effects that I didn't experience at all. But on the other hand, it could be that I will not have any of the side effects, so I have to be hopeful.
- Third, I have already prepared food that I found that I'm able to enjoy—that somehow are in the range of my taste experience that is either unaffected or less affected by the drug. Therefore, having those foods with me allows me not only to be calm, but also to know that I'm going to get adequate nutrition, assuming that I'm going to be able to eat those foods.
- Fourth, there's exercise. While I was at home over the past week I started to use some home-based exercise

---

1   The reason for this difference was purely due to space considerations in the oncology ward.

equipment—an exercise rubber band that allows me to do a number of exercises for my upper body and a spring that I use to exercise my chest and shoulders—and I decided that I'm going to start doing some stomach exercises as well. Having been active in a gym for around the last fifteen years, I am used to a basic level of exercise. I work out with weights, in addition to my regular aerobics exercise which I like to do outdoors. So, the outdoor aerobic exercise is very restricted, but we've been fortunate over the past few weeks to have nice weather, and Ricki and I have been going out for long walks.

I believe taking just those two pieces of equipment—the rubber band and the spring—with me to the hospital will be a very important psychological boost, and will give me an opportunity to do just a little bit more exercise, and that will be good for me.

That's a very good approach. I feel good. I feel strong. I feel fortunate to be able to receive more treatment that can lead to quicker and more complete eradication of the tumor, and get rid of this problem. In this case, the doctors want to do surgery as well. So this round of chemotherapy should increase the likelihood of a successful surgery, and *b'ezrat Hashem*, everything will work out well. At this point, I can honestly say I am looking forward to moving ahead with this treatment, and we will be beyond this problem, with God's help, within a few months.

DECEMBER 28, 2018/ 20 TEVET 5779

Ely Message for Shabbat *Shemot*

This Shabbat is quite an important Shabbat in my life and, really, in all of our lives. On the one hand, there's a reality on the ground. In a few hours, I'm going to be going into the hospital for five days of chemotherapy. We had one day as an outpatient yesterday. Thank God there were no problems. I'm feeling good.

But these next days might be more difficult, as I recall from a few weeks ago when I was admitted, and it was not so pleasurable.

But there's a lot to learn for me by looking at the story in this week's Torah portion, *Shemot*. These are the stories of our nationhood. These are the stories that are the basis for the Pesach celebration of the year, and the ultimate salvation that we talk about.

We can understand that there's **one plan**. God's plan was evident from the beginning. There's no other explanation. That's certainly the way it's told to us in the Torah, and that is how it unrolled. You have a plan that involved going into hardship and being oppressed and getting into a situation that is seemingly unresolvable by humans—and seems hopeless. But, indeed, it's all part of God's plan, for a purpose. He plans the antidote and the future *geulah* from Egypt together with the problem, by providing us with Moshe, the leader who eventually takes the Israelites out of Egypt and leads them to the doorstep of Israel.

No one could have known that ahead of time. But now, in hindsight, we can feel confident that God has our best interests in mind, though we certainly cannot understand how He works, or the rationale. I don't think there's anyone alive who can truly say that they understand why history had to be exactly as it is, in that the Jews had to go down to Egypt and be oppressed for so long and to work as slaves so long. But clearly, there are reasons, and sometimes with hindsight we can see the good in it. But when we're living through it, we often don't see the goodness in it because our ability to see that goodness is very limited. We don't even know what that goodness really means.

The Torah portion starts with a reminder of how we, as Jews, came to Egypt with full confidence that the family would eventually return to their land. But we are immediately told that the favorable environment that the Jews were given due to Joseph's prominence was quickly reversed and the king of Egypt, the Pharaoh, decided to enslave the Jews, treat them harshly, and oppress them. That was the situation for the Jews, and that's the way it was for many, many years. You had Jews who were born into slavery, and they died in slavery. Their sons and daughters were born into slavery, and they died in slavery. What kind of outlook could they possibly have on life? We know from our lives that we tend to think that what will be is based on what there is. In their situation, this seemed to have been proven out. So, they were always going to be slaves. There was never a future for them and their lives must have been quite depressing and hopeless. They had no way of revolting against the strongest country in the world at the time, and their ability to think beyond themselves (and certainly to connect with God) was quite limited under those circumstances.

But at the same time, we're told that the antidote was provided by God from the start. The ultimate vehicle of redemption—their future leader, Moshe—was born at the same time that the most severe oppressive policies were put into place. Moshe grows up, and he has to escape Egypt for killing a man. Now Moshe is in exile. Is it clear at all to us that this man has any role in the future of the redemption of Israel? Should anyone have hope? No. It's not obvious to him, it's not obvious to anyone.

The next thing we know is that he's eighty years old, tending his flock of sheep, and there's a whole encounter on Mount Horev, where God reveals to him that he is chosen to lead the people of Israel out of Egypt. He has all sorts of reasons why that shouldn't be, but God tells him, "No, no, no. It's you." God provides him with miraculous, unnatural, highly magical signs that he can provide to convince the people, and for Pharaoh to accept that he is God's messenger—that he is, indeed, the true leader. Sure enough, that's what happens.

The amazing thing (for me) is that we can now take a step back and have a high-level view of what's really going on here. What we're really seeing applies to all of us in our lives and especially to my situation.

Seeing the ultimate history allows us to fully relax, to fully have comfort in the fact that God has a plan, and His plan is good, and He has the power to execute that plan. He is the only One to Whom we can pray to help ease our conditions. We make sure that we are doing everything we can in our power to satisfy His will so that we can be *zocheh* to that redemption—and it's that comfort that is critical.

It is that comfort that allows us to have hope, and that is the seed of *geulah*. The greater we are in that thought, the happier we feel, the closer we feel to God. This positive feedback loop is present all the time the closer we are to God. Therefore, we're able to feel God's presence, we're more able to appreciate his plan, and then the closer we are to God. So we're able to become more and more calm, more and more happy. It's true even at a time of apparent darkness. May you be blessed with a *Shabbat Shalom*, and we should all be privileged to see the *geulah*.[2]

DECEMBER 30, 2018/ 22 TEVET 5779

Ricki Thoughts from the Oncology Ward, Round 2

We are in the middle of a chemotherapy treatment which is scheduled to last a total of six days. It is now Sunday, and we started last Thursday. We have been in the hospital since Friday.

It is really a challenge to keep our thoughts straight. Even though we've gotten pretty good at it, when you are staring at an IV pole pumping very strong chemotherapy medicine into your loved one, when you see people who are very sick and dying in adjacent rooms, it is tough not to think about the medical side of this. And the medical side is at the very least unpleasant, and at most very worrying. So once your brain starts taking you in that direction, it is a challenge to get out of that level of thinking. It

---

2   After sharing this piece with the rabbi of our synagogue, Rav Eli Reif, he wrote the following: God said to Moshe, "כי אהיה עמך—I will be with you." Moshe was a messenger, but not in the human sense, wherein the messenger is on a mission but the person sending him is not on the mission together with the messenger. In this case, God is the One sending him on the mission, but He is also *on* the mission together with Moshe. Moshe may not see Him, but He is there. In this phrase, "I will be with you," God is giving all of us a message—that He is with us on our paths, even though we cannot see Him.

requires climbing above the reality on the ground and seeing it from a different angle. This does not mean denying reality, but it does mean controlling the focus of our thoughts.

Ely and I both believe with all of our hearts that Hashem is actively part of our lives. We also believe with all of our hearts that Hashem is Good. If you put those thoughts together, then you *know* that everything that happens is deliberate and is for the ultimate Good. So I keep taking both of those thoughts, and drilling them in to my head more and more. I recently commented to Ely that the constant drilling going on across the way from our apartment (a new neighborhood is going up on the hill across from us) is really a drilling into my thick skull of the *bitachon* and the right thoughts that need to be there *all the time*. When I finally get that, the drilling will stop and the "buildings" will start to emerge—seemingly out of nowhere, but really from the foundation that was laid.

Just this morning, I had a moment of appreciation for the *hashgachah* that is always with me surrounding my work. I have been working as an independent patent agent, with my own clients, for fourteen years now. And it never fails. When I have more time, I have more work, and when I have less time, the workload somehow decreases. And somehow, even though my workflow is somewhat sporadic, it provides us with just enough income to keep us afloat. This does not just "happen." I have been aware of this pattern for a very long time, but the knowledge of this phenomenon has been something intellectual. The emotion that should go along with the awareness of this incredible, phenomenal "phenomenon" has been lacking. Today, sitting in the hospital, I received an email that allowed me to relax about a particular case that I thought would be a headache. At that moment, I started to appreciate this *hashgachah* at a different level. And as I am sitting here writing these words, tears are coming to my eyes. Because this is one more sign that we are being enveloped by Hashem's love. Through it all. Right in the heart of this difficult treatment, He is sending us signs that He is there with us.

We have to keep walking on the right path, keeping our thoughts straight, praying for a good outcome, and sharing our insights with others. With that, I feel protected.

DECEMBER 30, 2018/ 22 TEVET 5779

Ricki Ely's Uniqueness

Something that is popping out for me today is Ely's uniqueness. Some examples: at 5:30 a.m. he wanted to be disconnected from the IV so he could shower. The nurse was quite surprised by this request. "Now?" he asked.

Yes, that is Ely.

The social worker walked into the room and commented, "You are in your regular clothes!" She was surprised by this, because she is used to seeing patients in hospital gowns or at least in pajamas, and in bed.

Yes, that is Ely.

Last week, he was told that he is very organized. The basis for this statement was that Ely sends out WhatsApp updates to a list of people. He did not see why this made people think he was organized. I pointed out to him that he does not see it because that is just how he is.

Yes, that is Ely.

He doesn't appreciate his uniqueness, because it is just him. He is who he is. I understand him in a way that other people don't. I see him and I know that there is not an ounce of laziness, and not a moment of doubt. He is an *eved Hashem*, eager to fulfill his job in this world, with the full knowledge that Hashem is leading the way. He is totally modest about this and doesn't even recognize the seemingly small things that other people see and are amazed by. I too am humbled by his strength, by his outlook, and by his approach to this illness in particular.

I have the sense that people don't really know how to process this person that is Ely. But that is OK. He just needs to keep being himself. That is his job in this world. Now and forever.[3]

JANUARY 1, 2019/ 24 TEVET 5779

Ricki Bump in the Road

Ely is not doing so well today. He is very slow and weak, and he has fever too.

Am I worried?

Well, there is a part of me that is.

But mostly, I am in a good place today. I know with all of my heart that Hashem is Good and that the love He has for us is total and complete. So whatever we are going through right now is for a very, very good reason.

It is difficult to see him like this. He is miserable and there is nothing I can do to help him other than just be here. So I am here. I will do whatever I can to make him feel better, knowing that it is limited right now.

My *tefillah* today was slow and strong. I pray that Hashem have mercy on him and not let him suffer too much. I pray that we get past this so that we can do our work together for many years.

JANUARY 1, 2019/ 24 TEVET 5779

Ricki Get Off the Future Axis

I must get off the future axis and *stop worrying.*

The difficulty right now is that there is seemingly nothing else. We are in the hospital, surrounded by sickness, and Ely is feeling really, really lousy. I started to worry more because he is extremely tired, he keeps trying to get up and keeps falling asleep,

---

3   When I wrote this piece, I was not at all sure I would make it public because Ely would probably not have wanted me to. But now that he has passed away, I believe it is inspiring for others, and it is correct to include it here.

and he still has fever. He tried to get up a few times to get ready for bed, and he started shaking with chills. I called the nurse to check on him, and she asked the doctor to come and check. We are now waiting to hear if they plan to increase his antibiotics or not. But sitting here waiting while Ely drifts in and out of sleep with spurts of coughing, it is difficult to get off the future axis. In the past, I have done this by focusing on the current good. But the current situation does not feel good so I can't focus on that. What to do?

I tried to pray a bit. That would seem like a good thing to do at a time like this. But my prayers are focused on an outcome, which puts me back on the future axis.

So I sat down to write. Writing seems to help—a bit.

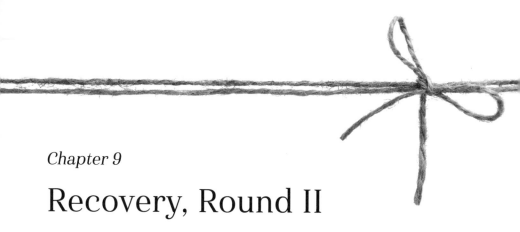

Chapter 9

Recovery, Round II

We were scheduled to finish the chemotherapy and leave the hospital on Tuesday, January 1, 2019 (24 Tevet 5779). But Ely caught the flu somehow and they kept him for a few more difficult days. Finally, it was time to go home and recover. The recovery this time was much more challenging, probably due to the complication of the flu, as well as the cumulative effects of the chemotherapy drugs.

JANUARY 5, 2019/ 29 TEVET 5779

Ricki Protecting the Kids

This has been a particularly difficult few days. We are finally home from the hospital, but Ely is quite weak and is still fighting the flu, with a terrible sounding cough. The challenge is to stay focused and not lose my faith in his recovery or the tremendous *chessed* that Hashem has been giving us.

One of the really difficult things for me is thinking about Tamar.[1] I know this is hard for her, but I don't fully understand what she might be thinking or feeling and how to help her. I also have a tendency to want to spare my children pain—save them from every scraped knee (and chipped tooth, as happened last

---

1   Tamar is the only one of my children who is also Ely's biological child, and she is the only one of Ely's biological children who is not yet an adult. As such, my focus in this regard was on her. Of course, all of the other children were greatly challenged by the situation as well.

week). But I have to constantly remind myself that I did not cause this situation for my child. Hashem did. So I have to know with absolute certainty that whatever trials my children may have, they are the right trials for them at the right times in their lives. It may be to help shape them into the people they need to be. It may be for other reasons which I don't fully understand. But I have to know my place here. I can help them cope, I can help soothe the pain, I can let them know that I am here for them, but I cannot change the situation and it is not helpful (and may be harmful) to try to protect them from their reality.

I know in my heart that my job as a mother is to love my children and to help them through their trials in life, but to know that I can't protect them from feeling pain or from the challenges they face in life. Some things are in my hands, but most things are not. This challenge really does test my *bitachon*, and takes it to a whole new level.

JANUARY 5, 2019/ 29 TEVET 5779

Ricki Teaching My Children

I have to take this opportunity to make sure that my children, and Tamar in particular, learn to think of others, to be appreciative for all that they have, and to develop their own *bitachon*.

I say particularly Tamar because she is only seven years old. She is a good girl, smart and caring, but like all seven-year-olds, she mostly is concerned with her own needs.

However, I need to know that she is not too young to develop a sense of caring for others. In fact, it is critical that she does so. I need to use this opportunity to teach her how to think outside of herself. How to offer a hand, or give a loving word, or even know when to seek my attention and when to let me be.

I also need to instill in her a sense of gratitude. She can walk around feeling sorry for herself. Or she can look at her life and see the good.

Finally, the *bitachon* is the trickiest part. How do you talk to a seven-year-old about *bitachon*? I can't just tell her everything will be OK. But she also needs to feel secure, and to know that there is a God that is watching over us.

I pray that Hashem gives me the insight and the understanding to know how to teach my children these important lessons during this trying time. Oh yeah, and how to teach myself as well...

JANUARY 17, 2019/ 11 SHEVAT 5779

 What (or Who) Is Responsible for Healing?

I underwent a second PET-CT test two days ago. This test is a sophisticated imaging test that combines the anatomical precision of the CT with the imaging of metabolic activity of the PET. Essentially, it shows the doctors where, and to what degree, there is tumor activity in my body. This morning, my oncologist called to tell me that my case was presented at the Tumor Board interdepartmental conference. There, the images were reviewed by the group of physicians, and the consensus emerged that the cancer shrunk a little, but there is still a considerable amount of tumor on the left side of my neck. The ENT (Ear Nose Throat) surgeons think it is operable, and therefore the conclusion of the conference was that the next step is to plan the surgery. I was asked to come to the hospital on Sunday morning.

I started to think about what is really responsible for the healing. There are so many factors that seem to be critical. But is it the chemotherapy drugs that may shrink the tumor, the PET-CT test that allows the doctors to precisely plan the surgery, the oncologist who has the expertise relating to radiation therapy and chemotherapy, or the surgeons who will operate to remove the remaining cancer? Is it the researchers whose work has resulted in all the advances that led to the current therapies? Is it the psychological factor—the maintenance of a positive attitude?

The answer, of course, is that all of these are important. But all are agents of the true healer, God. Even the oncologists and the surgeons, with all their combined skills and expertise, are human beings. The best they can do is to care and to try their best to apply the knowledge and skills to help me. Ultimately, they do not determine the outcome. In my view, they are messengers of God (whether or not they share that viewpoint), empowered with gifts to be applied to help me.

Their knowledge and clinical judgment are dependent on their cognitive facilities and the creativity that is a feature of the human mind. These functions of the brain and mind are at once the feature of nature that distinguishes humans from all other animals and gives us the abilities to endeavor to heal, and also makes us critically aware of the limitations of the human brain and mind. No matter how we try, our efforts seem primitive and are always associated with possible side effects. Simply put, we doctors do our best with the available tools to benefit our patients in the face of harm that may result; we just have to try to ensure that the benefits outweigh the risks.

The true healing occurs within our bodies in ways that modern science does not really understand. The "magical" healing powers of the body are relied upon by our doctors. After the surgeon cuts, he knows that the body will repair the wounds. After the oncologist administers the strong chemotherapeutic agents, she knows that the body will undergo healing that takes one or two weeks to return the patient to a reasonable level of functioning.

So what is the driving factor for this incredible built-in healing capacity, the impressive brain power of the doctors, the creativity of the researchers, etc.?

It is the Supreme Being.

JANUARY 17, 2019/ 15 SHEVAT 5779

Ricki No Complacency

I just read through all of our writings until now. I haven't written in a while, and I am now questioning whether that is a reflection of some slippage on my part. Have I started to lose some of the fire that I had at the beginning? Am I forgetting to look at every moment with wonder? To use my time in the right way? To try to incorporate more *chessed* into my life? To be fair, I have been more attuned to the needs of others than in the past. But I am not sure that I am completely on track. One thing I have to be absolutely sure about is that I do not let *complacency* settle in. That would be tragic. So it's time to refocus, to make sure that I am on track, and to keep on working.

My goal for the next few days is to focus on gratitude. And not just any kind of gratitude. I mean the kind of gratitude that brings tears to my eyes because it is so unexpected and just so good. The kind of gratitude that we should have all the time, that David Hamelech clearly had, as expressed in so many of his *Tehillim*. The kind of gratitude that just sings and soars.

JANUARY 17, 2019/ 15 SHEVAT 5779

Ricki When I Retire....

When I have a challenge in front of me, I have a very strong tendency to think that *after* the challenge is completed, I will be able to enjoy life. This can take many forms—it can be on a long time scale or a short time scale. It can be for a big challenge or for something relatively trivial. It can involve milestones that I have personally in my life, or it can involve milestones having to do with my children. No matter what the cause, I often find myself on this track of "after X, I will do/feel Y."

Well.

Today I started to have a thought like that, wherein the "event" that I had in mind was several years down the road. But then

I stopped in my tracks, and I remembered that the time frame of "several years" is something we can no longer relate to in a confident way. Who knows if we will be around in several years? Who knows what will happen between now and then? How can I possibly think about what I might do or how I might feel at a time that is so far away?

And then I remembered one of the big lessons of our current experience. We must embrace the present. We must be here, enjoying it, living it, making the decisions and doing the jobs that we need to do right now. We must feel good even in the midst of challenges. Not just the challenges of the illness we are faced with, but *all* of our challenges. Big and small.

Many people think, "When I retire, I will..." Does that mean that until they retire, they will not feel good? They will not relax, enjoy their families, enjoy their lives, and try to fill their time with good, productive activities? I hope not. And the same is true for the small difficulties that we face.

We need to focus on the present, feel good, and be the best versions of ourselves. Yes, even in the midst of it all.

Chapter 10

Planning for Major Surgery

We were told that the surgery would take place on January 30, 2019. It was clear to us that this would be a serious procedure—and a critical one as well.

JANUARY 21, 2019/ 15 SHEVAT 5779

Ely Faced with the Details of the Surgery

This is the message I sent today to the sixty or so people who are on my broadcast list, the people who have expressed the desire to be updated regarding my status:

> *Good morning. Today I have a big update. The surgery is scheduled for **next Wednesday, January 30th**. For more details, see below.*
>
> *Yesterday, Ricki and I went for a pre-surgical clinic visit consisting of evaluations by a nurse, an anesthesiologist, and a group of surgeons from the ENT department. We learned the following:*
>
> - *The planned surgery will involve two parts.*
>   - *A small area of the tongue, where the cancer started, will be removed. This is intended to*

include a margin of healthy tissue to make sure that they get out all of the cancer from the tongue. Because this is small, they do not expect any functional problems after the wound heals.

- *They will perform "surgical dissection" on the left side of my neck in order to carefully remove the tumor while leaving intact as much of the normal structures as possible. In principle, the surgeons will remove structures that have already been invaded by the tumor, and they will save the structures that have not been invaded. There may be cosmetic changes due to this—less bulk on the left side of my neck. They will try to minimize this.*

- *All told, they were confident about their ability to operate and to remove the cancer.*

• *The surgery is expected to last all day—about eight hours.*

• *After the surgery, I will be in a recovery ward for at least twelve hours. After they deem that I can be moved, I will be taken to an intensive care area of the ENT ward, where I may be for a few days. After that, I will be moved to a regular room on the ENT ward. We were told to expect to be in the hospital for around two weeks after the surgery.*

• *In all likelihood, I will not be able to talk or eat for the first ten days after the surgery. I will be fed by a tube that will go directly into my stomach. Once deemed appropriate, I will be allowed to start eating food, with gradual upgrades from soft foods to regular foods. After I can eat, I can be discharged home.*

• *Once home, it will still take around three weeks of recovery. So, I will be out of commission for around five weeks after the date of the surgery—around two weeks in the hospital and three weeks thereafter.*

- *Regarding visitation throughout, it is best to be in contact with Ricki.*

So, we know that the ENT surgeons are on the case, and they are planning a serious operation with good results. Recovery will take a long time. We remain confident in the surgical team's caring, judgement, and technical abilities.

Prayers may be directed to ask Hashem to guide these messengers and deliver a refuah sheleimah.

I find it important to keep those who care updated on the technical facts of my treatment. That way, Ricki and I do not need to talk too much about the medical details, and we can focus our interactions on positive and forward-thinking matters.

Now, you can ask: How am I dealing with this news? Indeed, there are two points of difficulty for me:

- The first is that the surgery itself carries risks of damage to nerves, muscles, and blood vessels.
- The second is that there will be a long recovery period.

To both of these points, my logical brain tells me that the purpose of this operation is to rid my body of cancer. All other considerations are relatively minor. My emotional brain starts to tell me that I should be scared or nervous, but then I remind myself that I am in good hands. The good hands are most visibly the doctors of the Beilinson ENT department, who have been consistently caring and professional. But, the true good "hands" behind the scene are those of Hashem. My trust in Hashem is the bedrock for my level of comfort and feeling that I am being cared for.

JANUARY 24, 2019/ 18 SHEVAT 5779

Ricki *Yad Hashem* – the Hand of God

One thing we knew immediately: this was *Yad Hashem*. It was so unusual, so unexpected, that we knew it could only be viewed through that lens. There is something about the unpredictable, highly unusual occurrences that causes us to see the workings of God. It is easier to see it when an unusually good event occurs. But my basic premise is that if we take our notion of good and bad out of the equation (not an easy task, but bear with me), the grandiosity or "wow factor" really stands out. Ideally, this feeling should be there in the regular events as well. But one thing is sure: when an unusual event happens, it should cause us to sit up and take notice. The more unpredictable or unusual it is, the more the Hand of God is apparent. Even with all that, it's been a struggle. Because we're fighting our human tendencies and previous thought patterns.

JANUARY 26, 2019/ 20 SHEVAT 5779

Ely Thoughts Going into Surgery

In just over two months since the beginning of this journey, I have undergone extensive diagnostic testing and two rounds of strong chemotherapy. Last week, Ricki and I were told that the consensus of the doctors was that a very long and delicate operation is required to carefully separate out the cancer from the healthy tissue, and to remove as much cancer as possible while minimizing damage to the normal tissues of my neck (i.e., muscles, nerves, blood vessels, etc.). We were also told that the doctors often recommend radiation therapy following such operations, to kill whatever cancer cells may have remained.

Now, with only four days until the surgery, I find myself thinking about how to cope. What should I be thinking? What should I be praying for? Should I worry about the details of a good outcome—when will this illness end, and when can I return to healthy functioning? Should I worry about the possibility of complications or a bad outcome?

How will I deal with the news I will receive from the surgeons about the success of the surgery and its implications for additional treatments and my ultimate prognosis? Will I learn any definitive information that can lead to conclusions about how this chapter in my life will end up? Do I even want to hear such projections, given that the surgeons' ability to predict outcomes in individual cases is limited and imprecise? Such predictive ability is based only on statistical data from large groups and from anecdotal data based on the personal experience of my doctors.

As I have expressed since the first day that I found out that there might be a serious illness, I have adopted a positive attitude. That statement, however, does not capture what is involved in combating the stream of negative thoughts that try to instill doubt, worry, and fear. I have shared how my Jewish belief system, my view of reality, and the positive reverberations from family and friends have consistently helped in my finding meaning, purpose, and hope through this trying time.

This, however, is a more extreme challenge:

- On the one hand, this operation is the most definitive and concrete way to remove cancerous tumor from the body. That is good.
- On the other hand, the operation itself poses risks, and there are no guarantees that the surgeons will be able to remove the whole tumor.

After giving this considerable thought, I have decided to view this issue in two ways:

- First, the question of the timeline—what to expect for the future?
- Next, the question of what to pray for—what help to ask for?

Timeline

Before the news of my illness, I was living a life that had many components, including family, work, and pleasure. I never considered myself as conforming to any particular model of normalcy, but outsiders would certainly consider my life path as one that would be expected to continue productively until some ripe old age.

This naïve view, of course, was shattered by the unexpected news that I am harboring a malignant tumor. We all know that life is fragile. We all know that people are killed suddenly by natural disasters such as hurricanes, traffic accidents, war and terrorism, and by severe illness. However aware we are of these life occurrences, we do not expect them to happen to us or our loved ones. When we can do something to treat the threat, we are eager to act. In my case, we have done all we can to rapidly diagnose the problem and to engage in treatments recommended by the experts.

We are now at the critical juncture—the run-up to the most definitive treatment. There is a tense suspense around the day of the surgery. It seems that I would expect to wake up in the recovery room and be told that all will be good. The trouble with this thought is that neither I nor the surgeons know what "good" means. What is the expected good that I want? Also, I am aware that the doctors do not issue guarantees for the future. What is the certainty of their determination of good? Further, will any hesitation or caveats regarding risks or news of potential disability destroy the image of good that I want to have? In short, I am not comforted by the bland reassurance that "it is all good."

The best and most truthful answer for me is that I cannot judge the goodness of the news I will receive because I do not know what a truly good outcome is. This is particularly true in the scope of the long term. I do not know how long I am supposed to live, and I have no idea of the impact of the cancer and its treatment on that determination. The only One who determines those matters is God.

Here is how my thinking goes: If I could request a specific outcome, what would I ask for? Would it be expressed in the length of time that I have to live, the quality of the life that I will have, or some other characteristic? Would it be to live to 120 or to request that I live until the current average expected lifespan of around eighty or some other number? Would I request that I be granted a certain expectation for quality of life (I am not sure how that could be expressed or measured)? Would I ask to be returned to my prior life path or some different level of functioning? For sure, the answer is that I would not ask for any specific outcome. On the one hand, asking for a specific lifespan or quality of life would only limit me. How do I know that I should not ask for an even longer lifespan or a better quality of life? On the other hand, I have no basis for any expectations for what should be. The clear answer for me is to ask that I receive whatever outcome God has in store for me. That is, I will pray to God for Him to deliver whatever lifespan and quality of life He wants for me. Since His Will is connected to the merit of my devotion to and execution of His Will, I will also pray that I merit the best possible outcome in His view.

It may be comforting to "know" what is going to be in the end, but the only relevant question in that regard is whether I will survive past the immediate threat to my life caused by the cancer, or whether I will not. To start, this is a difficult question. The only "end" we can all be certain of is that we will all die at some time—and we have no idea as to when that time will come. Nonetheless, we have certain expectations regarding lifespan, and we would like to think that each of us reach or exceed that age. In my case, we have been told by the doctors that there is no evidence that the cancer has spread beyond my neck to the rest of my body. That is, of course, very good news. That gives me a sense of confidence regarding survival. Yet, there are many unknowns.

I find it much more relevant to go step by step. It is most important to learn about the results from each test and each treatment, and how that step influences the thinking of my doctors. I do not need to know "what will be" in the end. As I said, only God has that vision. However, I do need to be fully advised of the medical facts and the associated opinions of the doctors. In that way, I am prepared for all shades of prognosis. No matter what information and opinions are presented, it will always be in the context of the "best available information" and the "best and current recommendations of the doctors." There are no guarantees about the future—just the best opinions that our human doctors can provide. The big picture will not change; I am in God's hands and am fully prepared to accept His Will, no matter whether or not the current facts and projections appear to me as good.

What to Pray For

Now, I want to turn to the question of what to pray for. I conceptualize our ecosystem as having four "players." There are the doctors, family and friends, me and Ricki, and Hashem in the center. It works like this:

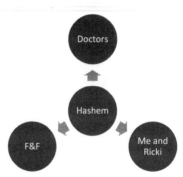

- The doctors' job is to try their best. They are the messengers. I pray for Hashem to give them wisdom, correct judgement, the creativity to improvise, proper mood, and the most conducive circumstances.
- Ricki and I are undergoing trauma. I will be under the knife and will need to recover from physical trauma. Ricki is under considerable stress and will need to recover from psychological trauma. I pray for Hashem to give each of us

the strength to endure and recover from the trauma of the cancer and the operation. I further pray that He delivers complete healing and repair in the way that no human can.

- Our family and friends are so helpful, as the *chessed* they deliver has empowered us with positivity and hope. The love, support, caring, and physical help are important in ways that cannot be measured. I pray for Hashem to give our support network the focus and strength to provide positive support and proper prayers. I further pray that the strength that we get from our family and friends may be reflected back to them and that they may be strengthened by our positive energies.

- In the center is Hashem—God. I pray for God to continue to shower His love upon us, to make our will the same as His Will, to give us the clarity of mind to know what thoughts and actions are best at every step, and to guide us on the road to improvement and growth. My highest prayer is that this challenge be used as an opportunity to move higher in our connection and devotion to Him.

Chapter 11

Surgery

Ely was admitted to the hospital the night before the surgery to make sure that everything was in place and that the surgery could start first thing in the morning. A full day of waiting was in store for the rest of us. Many of his family members, including his children, brother, and parents, came to wait and pray and be together during this time.

JANUARY 30, 2019/ 24 SHEVAT 5779

Ricki *Tefillot*

It is 8:20 a.m. on the day of the surgery. Ely was taken in to the operating room before 7:00 a.m., but the screen that is supposed to update us says he is in prep. I have been getting many messages, and I sent out a *Tehillim* link to all of our friends and family.[1]

Let me try to get my thoughts on paper. On the one hand, I am just waiting for a medical procedure to start and end. Not just any medical procedure, mind you. This is major surgery, and we don't really know what the outcome will be. But we do know there will be a difficult recovery.

---

1 *Tehillim*, or Psalms, are commonly said at times like this, when people want to come together to pray for someone. The "link" I am referring to is a system whereby the entire book of Psalms is available on a chapter-by-chapter basis. When someone clicks on the link, he or she receives a chapter to say. This is done until the entire Book is completed, at least once.

I want to remember how it felt to talk to Ely yesterday. It's going to be a while before we can talk again.[2] Not being able to have our high-level conversations is going to be very difficult. I miss him already. I am feeling emotional and I'm trying to parse out the feelings. To identify them.

I feel like this is a mini Yom Kippur. I felt that way during *tefillah* this morning. There is something very high and spiritual about this day. This is the day that Hashem has planned to remove this invader from Ely's body. Our *rav*, Eli Reif, wrote (translation): "Blessings and success with the operation today. My heart, thoughts, and prayers are for the success of the operation and the healing of Ely. May it be His will that from Heaven will he be accompanied, that with God's help the operation will be successful and that we will hear good news and full recovery. Be strong and courageous."[3]

Those words were very meaningful to me.

So what am I feeling?

Gratitude for Hashem's presence in our lives. Always.

Gratitude for our friends and family who are so loving and supportive.

Enveloped and embraced.

Somewhat weepy.

Missing Ely. Already.

I thought I would be able to write, but it's not flowing yet.

May the healing powers of God above flow through the hands of the surgeons into Ely, and may all of the evil be uprooted.

---

2   Comment by Ricki on June 2: I had no idea when I wrote that piece that it was the last time I would ever have a fully verbal conversation with Ely again. After the surgery, there was damage to one of his vocal cords. While the doctors thought it could be treated, the plan was to wait until after all of the cancer treatments.

3   In the original Hebrew:

ברכה והצלחה בניתוח היום. ליבי, מחשבתי, ותפילתי להצלחת הניתוח ולרפואתו של אלי ויהי רצון
שמן השמיים יסייעו ובעז"ה שהניתוח יעבור בהצלחה ונשמע בשורות טובות. רפואה שלמה. חזקי
ואימצי. אלי רייף

He is here as a total servant of Hashem. His attitude and out-look has already had such a profound effect on so many people.

It seems that my thoughts are pretty scattered today.

I just received an unbelievable message from my cousin after reading Ely's last piece. She said that she just read what Ely wrote[4] and that it was the most alive and effective lesson in *emunah* that she can ever remember. There are tears in my eyes.

---

4   On January 26/ 20 Shevat: "Thoughts Going into Surgery."

Chapter 12

Post-Surgery

After the surgical procedure, Ely was taken to recovery and then up to the ENT ward. Knowing that it would be an exhausting day, Ely's parents booked two rooms in an adjacent hotel for the night: one for them and one for me. I was extremely grateful for this gift, and once the surgery was over, and we had been informed that it was successful, we grabbed a bite to eat, returned to the recovery ward to see him for a few minutes, and then collapsed in the hotel. Although I expected to sleep soundly due to my exhaustion, in fact, I was unable to relax and I was tossing and turning for most of the night. Anxious to return to check on him, I checked out as early as possible and made my way back to the hospital before 7:00 a.m. Incredibly, Ely was already wide awake and in good spirits. During the course of the day, he managed to get up and walk around, and when he was not walking around, he insisted on sitting up in a chair rather than lying in bed. I was amazed by his quick physical recovery.

For two weeks after the surgery, Ely was not allowed to eat or talk. He had a feeding tube inserted through his nose, and he communicated by white board or computer. At the end of two weeks, when he was allowed to start eating and talking, it started to become clear that it would not be so simple. Eating was still a chore due to the sensitivity of his tongue. When he tried to talk, it became apparent that he was only able to talk at the level of a whisper. It later became clear that one of his vocal cords had been paralyzed—temporarily we hoped.

FEBRUARY 3, 2019/ 28 SHEVAT 5779

Ely Feeling Thankful and Humbled

Today is the fourth day after the operation, and it is the first time that I feel I can communicate my thoughts after this huge event. It is hard to wrap my brain around the enormity of what happened. According to the surgeons, they managed to remove all the tumors from my tongue and from my neck. The source of the cancer was a small area on the side of my tongue, and the doctors verified that they removed all of the cancer with enough margin of healthy tissue to be sure they got it all. That is the first good news.

Regarding my neck, this was apparently no ordinary operation. We knew that lymph nodes can be the clearing house for all types of inflammation, including cancer. And the large lymph node in my neck was the ominous sign that led to the cancer's discovery and was visible to observers. However, the cancer in my neck that the surgeons saw was so invasive that it "attacked" anything in its path—muscles, nerves, my jugular vein, and even impinged on my carotid artery (the major source of blood supply to my brain). They needed to painstakingly remove the cancerous tissue from the healthy structures, and they managed to remove it as one mass. Miraculously, these talented and dedicated doctors saved nerves and muscles that are important for movement of my head, arms, shoulders, and tongue. And, they also removed the threat to the carotid artery. The fact that the jugular vein was engulfed by the tumor and had to be removed is not of much concern, as other veins already have provided enough venous blood flow to the area. Further, the muscle that turns the head, the sternocleidomastoid, was also attacked by the cancer; however, the surgeons managed to save enough of this muscle so as not to require them to perform another procedure to bring a different muscle in its replacement. This was the best report that could be expected under the circumstances.

Thank God. And thank the doctors. Let's not forget the nurses and the rest of the medical staff. It is nothing short of a miracle that these humans were given the cognitive abilities—skills, judgment, creative improvisation, and more—to successfully manage such a challenge in the face of the pressure of knowing that my life depended on it. Even more remarkable is their compassion, dedication, kindness, and other moral characteristics that drive them to care for me as if I were their only patient. I am humbled.

As Jews, we are educated to care for people in need, and there are many specific directives to that end in the Torah. As a physician, I have dedicated my professional career to helping others. What we have witnessed here, however, seems to go beyond professional duties. I have learned much from Professors Spitzer and Bachar and the other doctors of the Ear, Nose, and Throat Department at Beilinson.

Just one week ago, I reflected on my thoughts going into the surgery. Now, on the other side of the surgery, my thoughts have not changed. My body still has a lot of recovering to do. We still have no guarantee about my future health. The human messengers have done their part, with the help and guidance of God.

Our wonderful and devoted family and friends have done much to provide positive support and to summon God's help through massive prayer campaigns—for that I am duly humbled and forever grateful. Ricki and I have no words to express the awe that we feel at the *chessed* being offered and delivered on a regular basis. What is behind this is the command that we mimic God in His kind and compassionate ways—even when there is nothing personal to gain. It may seem humanistic, possibly even the expected normal behavior, but it is not. We are not born with the desire to help others—we are rather educated by general society to fend for ourselves, even to the extent of survival of the fittest. But the values that are taught via the Torah for thinking about and performing many of God's commandments lead us to the ideals of kindness, equality, respect, and justice. To see these in practice as acts of *chessed* has been a grand learning experience for us.

Ultimately, Ricki and I are humbled by God's goodness. Although we are still in the thick of post-operative recovery and there may be additional treatments (e.g., radiation therapy) needed in the future, we can feel the growth that we are experiencing due to this challenge.

FEBRUARY 3, 2019/ 28 SHEVAT 5779

Ricki Chessed

It is hard to keep track of all of the unbelievable *chessed* that we are the recipients of. It completely overwhelms me to see how caring people are, and the things that they think of to help us. Starting with the paid professionals. True, this is their job. But really, we feel that many of the people who have cared for Ely go above and beyond. To start, they have chosen caring professions. Especially the nurses and aides, who have to deal with so many different aspects of illness—from relieving pain, to collecting and changing various forms of body fluid, to helping position the patient comfortably. I have a newfound respect for these wonderful, caring people.

Then there are the doctors, some of whom have spent extra time making sure we don't have any more questions, or just checking up on Ely to see how he is doing.

Family members have been there to help in any way needed—from rotating in the hospital, to taking care of Tamar, to providing food, and just for emotional support.

And then there are the caring people of our community—some of whom we are friends with but many whom we don't even know.

Just a few examples: a person who just barely knows Ely from *shul* gave my son a ride to school this morning. Two complete strangers gave me a ride to and from the hospital. Two incredible women have taken it upon themselves to make sure I and the children are taken care of. A high school girl slept over at our house to care for our seven-year-old while I was at the hospital overnight. Countless people, many of whom I don't even know, have cooked and delivered meals for us. The rabbi of our *shul* not only provided an answer to Ely's question about how to communicate on Shabbat without speaking, he himself went out and bought a magnetic board for Ely to use.

I am truly humbled.

FEBRUARY 4, 2019/ 29 SHEVAT 5779

 Why Am I Not Asking "Why"?

In recent conversations, I have become aware that many people consider it normal to ask "why." Why did this terrible disease happen to me? Why did I warrant this? Why me? To put this into a more familiar phrase: Why do bad things happen to good people?

They expect me to harbor a certain anger about why this "fate" has befallen me (assuming that I think that I am a good person). And, if so, they want to be able to comfort me or suggest professional help to ease my anguish.

It may come as a surprise, therefore, that I am not asking "why" and do not harbor any associated anger. Why am I not asking "why"?

There are a number of important points:

- First, I am not in control of outcomes, even though I have control of my decisions.
- Second, I am not wise or privileged enough to know all the rules of reward and punishment, and therefore I cannot judge the fairness of my situation.
- Third, it is interesting to note that people ask the question of "why" when bad things happen, but they readily accept that they deserve the good things that happen.
- Finally, the real question to be asked is not "why," but "for what purpose"?

The simple answer to my acceptance of my disease is that I am not so wise to know what to expect of life in the first place. In my life, I try to do what I can to better myself and my family, but I cannot determine any of the important outcomes. Health is a big topic, where we feel enabled to follow habits that can promote longer life or better quality of life. But we are all aware of the fragility of our health. You may seem healthy and strong one day, and the next day be bedridden with the flu, unable to walk due to a knee or hip problem, or disabled due to head trauma from a car accident. In my case, I was feeling fine and tried my best to stick to a healthy lifestyle; yet, I was unknowingly harboring a malignant tumor for some time. We are simply not in control of such things. That is the first point.

Even though I try to do what is right, it would be arrogant to think that I "deserve" a better set of happenings in my life. I cannot judge the correctness of such happenings, since I cannot know all the complexities of how such things are determined, and I do not have the Divine perspective to know what is truly good for me. So, who determines my health? That is the essence of the matter. There are essentially three ways to think about this:

1. Randomness
2. Fate
3. Divine providence

Let's consider these:

1. If I thought that all events in my life were random and senseless, then I would be in despair because that belief claims that no one is in control.
2. If I thought that all events in my life were strictly deter-mined by some "fate," then I might get angry and hopeless at being given such a fate without any power to change that fate or to help myself.
3. However, I firmly believe that all events in my life are much more complex—the big picture is controlled by God, but I also have the ability to choose my thoughts and

actions and to do what I think is right. If so, it is God's wisdom that determines the correctness and goodness of all things. His wisdom is so great as to create living creatures, universal physical laws, and human beings with such complexities that we (humans) cannot even think of creating something similar. So, I am happy to rely on His wisdom and to be left without all the answers.

We judge happenings in lives as "good" or "bad" depending on the time of judgment and on the perspective of the one making the judgment. For example, winning the lottery is generally judged to be good at the time, but is known to have destroyed many lives. While a windfall of cash can be exactly what you have wished for all your life, having that cash can lead to destruction of relationships, warped values, and wasting of the cash itself on unnecessary commodities. In retrospect, the event of winning the lottery may turn out bad.

In contrast, events that are first seen as "bad," such as losing your job, dealing with serious illness, or a lost business deal, may lead to personal growth and better outcomes in the future. These are then viewed as "good." So, I must conclude that my illness presents serious challenges at present but may very well lead to positive growth and a better future.

As a minor point, I have noted that most people have very asymmetric expectations from life. They are willing to accept good things that befall them, such as a new business opportunity or an unexpected introduction to a new life partner, and do not ask "why" such good things have befallen them. Rather, bad events are easy targets for judgment and negative feelings. I suppose this is built into the human way of thinking, but it defies the logic of fairness.

The most important takeaway from this discussion is that I view challenges in life as opportunities for growth, much in the way that the Austrian psychiatrist and famed Auschwitz survivor, Viktor Frankl, has written about. Together with Ricki, I have found that my sudden confrontation with cancer has refocused my priorities and has sharpened my thinking about the most important questions in life. My relationships are being strengthened with myself, family, friends, and God. I have no doubt that the positive outweighs the negative.

In the final analysis, I can no better ask the question "why did this happen to me?" than "why is my treatment going well and why do I feel stronger every day?"

I am appreciative for the goodness that I am given. That's all.

FEBRUARY 5, 2019/ 30 SHEVAT 5779

Ely   Six Days Post-Surgery

I am not allowed to talk or eat until ten days after the surgery. That is because the surgeons want my tongue to heal; remember, they removed part of it.

Let's pause and understand the importance of the fact that only a small volume of the tongue was removed. Had the cancer on the tongue been larger, there would have been a need to take a piece of muscle from somewhere else in my body to replace the missing tongue muscle. This would have meant a longer and more complex operation, as well as a longer and more difficult recovery period. Thank God that only a small piece of the tongue was cancerous. But, as Ricki mentioned today to me, it is truly remarkable. The doctors had commented on how unusual my case is. Usually, the primary tumor is larger and the secondary tumor is smaller than in my case. For some reason, I had a very small area of cancer on the tongue that then spread very aggressively to my neck. As we do not understand the reasons for any of these facts, we are left marveling at the success of the surgery and thanking God.

Now, back to describing the actual difficulties that I am experiencing and how I am dealing with them physically and emotionally. To explain this properly, I must describe the present physical and emotional difficulties as well as the psychological shock at the realization of what actually happened and how it may have turned out less well.

Now, six days after the surgery, I have a clear enough mind to fathom the danger I was in. Some who have read my account of the surgery have reflected to me the shock that they experienced on realization of the dangerous situation I was in. I must say that I did not feel this shock, and I still do not. Why not?

The short answer to my coping with the danger is that, for me, nothing has changed from my perspective that I had before the surgery. I always knew that I am in God's caring hands, that this whole disease is His doing, it is here for a purpose, and I would be saved if it was His will to save me. The description of the surgery does seem scary, but no scarier than it was according to the knowledge I already had. The total trust in God's control and His goodness is the only way for me to view this. Indeed, my security in the future is totally based on this approach. After the fact, I can only marvel at the miracles that God has delivered and thank Him profusely for His kindness.

My present difficulties are primarily the prohibitions on talking and eating. I communicate sparsely, using a whiteboard and a computer. It is hard to accept visitors when I am awake and aware but cannot carry on a conversation with them. Regarding eating, I am being fed a liquid mixture called Jevity that has a balance of needed nutrients and calories. To bypass my mouth, the Jevity feedings are pumped down a thin tube that goes from my nose to my stomach. This is certainly not the most pleasurable way to eat, but that's the way it is. Then, there is the feeding tube itself, which is a nasogastric tube called a "zunda" here in Israel, hanging out of my nose. Not the most attractive way to present myself. Finally, there have been occasional pains in my neck and head, and these have been treated with mild painkillers. By the way I am describing these matters, you can tell that they are all minor in my eyes. Why?

My present difficulties are temporary and pale in the perspective that my life was just saved. Here, too, I can have no complaints. The doctors and nurses take precautions to limit the chances of major complications. The minor, albeit anti-social, inconveniences that I need to deal with until my tongue is sufficiently healed, can be managed. The fact that the body can heal itself is so wondrous that it, too, brings my thoughts and emotions back to focus on the miracles at work.

FEBRUARY 8, 2019/ 3 ADAR I 5779

Ely Challenge to Recovery

It is now around three in the morning on the ninth day after the surgery. I have been having trouble sleeping, typically waking in the early hours. So here I am writing some thoughts that are running around in my head.

My recovery has been going very well. The only reason I am still in the hospital is due to the time that Professor Spitzer wants to give the tongue to heal prior to reinstating eating. I am receiving all my nutrition via tube feeding, and I am prohibited from talking, humming, or using my mouth to make any noise whatsoever. However, the stitches are out, all medications have been stopped, and my strength has been coming back. There is minor weakness in some muscles, and that is being helped by exercises that the physical therapist taught me. With that, I have been accepting more visitors—both family and friends who have asked to visit me in the hospital.

Sounds good. So what is the problem? I have experienced that the real obstacle to recovery is psychological, not physical.

It is generally good to receive support, but such support is not always positive and may actually pose obstacles to recovery. We should reserve the word "support" for interactions that help, and some other word should be used for interactions that have negative effects.

I have been trying to establish and maintain a positive attitude and have been actively projecting that attitude to family and friends. This is not only to advise them of my own approach, but also to help them cope with the situation. Due to the difficulties I am undergoing and the challenges to my attitude, it is not always possible for me to project positivity. But, when the feelings are true, I try to share them with others. If I were to project the negative feelings that I sometimes have, including fear and doubt, then it would be harder for others to feel positive.

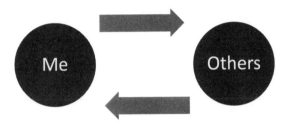

On the other side of the loop is the effect others' attitudes have on me. If the attitude is positive, then it helps me cope and stay positive. However, if the other's attitude is negative (or sufficiently more negative than mine), then it easily brings me down.

The ramifications are manifold, since this system is not a one-way road. It is a cycle, where we feed back to each other all the time. Positivity leads to more positivity; negativity leads to more negativity. So, the first point here is that both my attitude and that of the family member or friend are critical for both of us. The second point is that it does not just stop there. The influence of one on the other quickly feeds back to have further influence. Positive attitudes cause further positivity; negative attitudes cause further negativity.

What is a negative attitude in this context? The enemy here can wear many masks and seems always ready to pounce (a form of *yetzer hara*, if you will). Commonly, people are obsessed with "what if" situations: "What could be if?" and "What could have been if?" Even now, where in my case the treatments and recovery seem to be going well, I am hearing a lot of statements like, "I can't stop thinking about how this could have been much worse."

Then the worry is, "What (horrors await us) next?" Why is this negative; isn't it true?

Here's the catch: Even though there is some truth to both worries about the past and worries about the future, neither is actually true—and they are the wrong things to think about. The past was characterized by what was, not by what could have been. What happened resulted from many factors beyond our understanding and beyond our control. If, in hindsight, you realize that you had been saved from a much worse outcome, then your response should be one of relief and gratitude to God for having saved you. The future has not yet happened, and therefore may be influenced by your decisions as well as many other factors either unknown to you or out of your control. It is not right to worry about the future as if it were some impending disaster. Rather, your trust in God is needed to keep you relaxed and secure.

For example, if you drove home from work across a bridge, and then found out that the bridge collapsed a short while after you had been there, what should your thoughts be? Should you break down in anxiety and depression, or should you thank God for the fact that you were saved? The clear fact is that you were not meant to be on the bridge at the time of its collapse. It turned out that way and no other way. Now, going forward, should you worry every time you cross a bridge? Of course not. Your job is to go about your business with reasonable precautions. Having done your part, there is no more you can do. The rest is in God's hands.

Getting back to the feedback loop between me and my close relations (people who really care), it is important to emphasize the influence that we have on each other. If one of us is fearful and in despair, he implicitly assumes that the other has the same fears and despair. The dialogue between us will not be healthy for the one who is actually feeling happy, grateful, and positive about the future. It will bring him down. Conversely, if positivity and security in the future is the mood of the conversation, then it will serve to help the fearful one to see the situation from a different angle. The trick is that the feelings expressed need to be genuine, not a mask.

In my analysis, the critical difference between true positivity and negativity is always the degree of trust in God's providence—*bitachon*. That is the hidden, and most important, ingredient in one's attitude. This requires a very high level of belief that God is in control and that He is always good. With that, you can feel you are being cared for.

It is simply not enough to repeat the phrases "*Baruch Hashem*," "Thank God," or something similar. You have to strongly believe that that is how the world works. You have to *know* that God is ultimately in control, and that His will is good. With those two factors, there is nothing to worry about and there is every reason to feel secure in the future. You must know that God's love is real and constant even though you cannot understand it.

In our scientific age, we are schooled to think that we can trust only what we can see, or at least what we can measure. Yet, there are many things you cannot measure and you know that they are real. You surely have felt love in the past and know that it is real, even though there is no way to measure it. You can be confident that you will feel love in the future.

FEBRUARY 10, 2019/ 5 ADAR I 5779

Ricki Why the Break?

It's been a long time since I've written anything, and I've been asking myself why. Somehow, over the last week and a half since the surgery, I haven't really been able to connect to how I am feeling. Maybe it's exhaustion, maybe it's the underlying stress. I don't really know.

The interesting thing is that there seems to be a very large disconnect right now between my "logical" brain and my subconscious. If you were to ask me, "How are you doing?" my truthful answer would be that I am doing fine. I have (mostly) positive thoughts, I am thankful that the surgery went as well as it could have, relieved that there were no unexpected surprises or major debilitating after-effects.

And yet, my body is telling me that I am very stressed. I have this bone-tired exhaustion which can't be explained just from the trips back and forth to the hospital, I have a greater-than-usual need for chocolate or other sweet snacks, and I seem to be lacking the emotion that I would think/hope would go along with the positivity and thankfulness that I truly do have. I haven't been able to write at all. Strangely, at certain points in time I get weepy and I can't tell you why.

So here I am, trying to make sense of all of this. When I talked to Ely about this, he explained that we have been through a trauma and we are still recovering. True.

But I am still grappling with this disconnect that I know is there. I do think I have a tendency to cover up my strong emotions, only to have them burst out at certain unexpected moments. At some point in my training as a life coach, I realized that it is important for me to try to connect daily with what I am feeling. So for a few days I performed the following exercise: in the early morning hours, I would sit with a pad of paper and try to identify feelings that I was having—to put them into words. It didn't matter if they were logical or not or if I knew what was causing them or not. The point was to identify and name them as best as I could. This was not a simple task, and each time I did it, I was surprised by what I found. I think that has to be the formula for me during this time. At least for the next few days, I will try this exercise, and we will see what happens.[1]

---

1   I was unable to complete even this task.

Chapter 13

Going Home

The two weeks in the hospital went by, and then, thankfully, it was time to go home.

FEBRUARY 12, 2019/ 7 ADAR 1 5779

 The Trauma of Coming Home

We arrived home yesterday after thirteen days in the hospital. Immediately, the adrenalin was pumping in my veins as I excitedly reacquainted myself with our home. I went through the refrigerator looking for foods that I could try eating, given that I am still retraining to eat normal foods; it started with soft foods and is progressing to all foods.

I want to go back to my usual home routine. But...

Not so fast. That is my problem. I awoke today with a stark reminder of the harsh reality. I had pain on the entire left side of my neck and head. I was not comfortable, and I felt even worse than I did when I was in the hospital. What happened?

Ricki reminded me that I had undergone significant surgery and that it was undoubtedly very traumatic. I will take more time to slowly recover. My eagerness to assume my normal life routine was premature. For me, it is traumatic to come home, with all the cues of normal life around me. It seems I automatically assumed that I would be able to do more than I can actually do at this point. Did I overextend myself yesterday? I do not know. But for sure my psychological state suffered some trauma when faced with the discrepancy between my desires and my exhausted physical state. That was then reflected in the increased muscle tension and feelings of pain in my neck and head.

Here's what I am doing to adjust to this issue. With difficulty, I am following Ricki's advice and learning to override my desire for activity. I awoke today with the thought that I must go visit my uncle and aunt in Jerusalem. I am very close with them and have not seen them in several months. I seemed to think that it would not be a problem to drive forty-five minutes each way to see them. While in the area, we would also stop by to see my parents, who were planning on traveling to Modiin later in the day—so we could save them the drive. That, of course, is my fantastical idea of my physical state, ignoring the need for frequent rest. I must remind myself that I just returned home from the hospital yesterday, and that I am still in the throes of recovery from the severe physical trauma of surgery. Add to that the difficulty in eating: each meal for me is like a full workout at the gym.

I now realize that I must take it easy these next few weeks, with a slow buildup in activity. However difficult for me psychologically, my physical recovery demands it. So we are staying home. Now, to go for a short walk, come back and rest. And that is just fine. After all, I stopped all clinical and business activities so that I could be free to concentrate on recovering.

Let's see how it goes...

FEBRUARY 13, 2019/ 8 ADAR I 5779

 Post-Op Care in the ENT Department

We arrived home two days ago, and I have had time to reflect on the care I received for the twelve days after the operation when I was on the ward of the Head and Neck department (another term for the ENT department) at Beilinson Hospital. What was the level of care?

We all hear stories—mostly complaints—about the hospital care in the US and in Israel. We also hear scary warnings about hospital-borne infections and errors involving incorrect dosages of medications or even treatments administered to the wrong patients. Beilinson is a hospital that is administered by Kupat Cholim Clalit as part of the public health system. It is affiliated with Tel Aviv University Medical School, so it is also a major teaching hospital.

In a word, the care was good. Was it perfect? No. But, that is OK. The care from the doctors, the nurses, and support staff was solid. The ward has a pleasant feel, it is generally quiet and calm, and there is a feeling that all is under control.

The doctors came on rounds twice a day and were led by the senior ENT doctors. The group also consisted of residents and interns. The doctors monitored the healing of the surgical wounds, as well as the functions of my tongue and neck muscles. I did not have special needs and there were no complications, so I cannot say how the doctors would perform under those conditions. However, I have no reason to doubt that they would perform well.

The nurses at the times of shift changes were well-briefed about the doctors' plans and the nursing needs. They seemed to be organized for cooperative care—there was always a nurse assigned to my care, but other nurses would sometimes appear to help. When I called the nurse for some non-emergent need, such as to initiate tube feeding, response time was variable. In all cases, the job got done. Nurses were pleasant to deal with and seemed knowledgeable and skilled.

A physical therapist came by regularly to assess my strength and direct me with exercises. A dietician followed my caloric and protein intake. The support staff included nurses' aides, cleaning help, and others. They were also pleasant and effective.

Overall, my assessment is positive. Post-operative care was administered in a professional manner, and there were no complications. I have nothing to complain about. Well-done!

FEBRUARY 13, 2019/ 8 ADAR I 5779

Ricki   Disconnect

I have some further insights about the disconnect between my cognition and my emotions. I realized that I generally like to think positively, and that I see myself as an optimistic person. I also do truly believe that God is in charge. So what happens when I am faced with something negative, including a negative emotion, is that I tend to whitewash it. I tell myself that everything is good, and cognitively give myself reason to believe that. I think this at least partially stems from pressure that I put on myself to be good, to react well, to live up to my vision of myself. The problem is that this does not allow for true acceptance of negative emotions or events. It does not allow for sadness, grief, worry, or even fear (although that one still has a strong hold and tends to break through my defenses). I also think of myself as internally honest, but I realized that this tendency that I have is not intentional but prevents me from having complete and true internal honesty. This sometimes can result in a type of depression, where I start to lose touch with the true positive feelings. So I have to stop putting pressure on myself to feel a certain way and start getting in touch with my true emotions in real time, so that I can face them head-on and clear the way to feel as good as my cognitive brain is telling me I should be feeling. And I can't be hard on myself or impatient when that doesn't happen. I just have to be true to myself.

FEBRUARY 14, 2019/ 9 ADAR I 5779

Ely My First Mini-Crisis

I woke up this morning in a troubled state. Since returning home three days ago, I have been feeling more and more tension and pain around the left side of my neck and head. Eating is a chore, and no food that I have eaten since I was allowed to start eating four days ago has been enjoyable. My tongue seems clumsy and cannot easily push the food around my mouth to facilitate chewing and swallowing. I have started talking a little, but I am aware that too much talking strains my tongue. It seems like I am not getting better.

To make matters worse, I awoke in the middle of the night in severe pain and a cold sweat. The troubling thought that came to me was "Will I ever recover?" This thought was not dominant, but its very existence was a shock to me.

I must emphasize that my doubt was very slight and temporary, and that it did not seriously challenge my trust in God. Still, it is important to understand the train of thought that resulted in shock, why it posed a mini-crisis, and how I overcame it. I realize that similar thoughts abound when people are challenged with life's troubles, so my struggle may be helpful to others. Of course, these same thoughts could also pose threats to my mental health in the future. So here is my analysis.

The thought of "Will I recover?" is not merely a rational question that can be pondered based on the medical statistics.

On the one hand, we were told that recovery could take up to five weeks from the time of the surgery, and there are small chances of complications such as bleeding, infections, and other less frequent problems.

On the other hand, we saw other patients who underwent similar operations with different problems with recovery. One caregiver reported that a second operation is required for his wife due to the fact that some of the internal surgical wounds "did not close," and another patient, who published a YouTube video about her experience, discussed how it took over five months for her to recover.

The current problem, however, is an existential question that digs deep into my faith and core beliefs. Since this journey has started, I have managed to keep a strong connection to my inner knowledge of the controlling Hand of God and the trust that I may place in Him to carry me through this challenge in the best way, as defined by Him. With that, I feel cared for. I never had a question that implied hopelessness or despair.

Now, for the first time, some doubt raised its ugly head.

For me, this was a mini-crisis.

I must explain why I see "Will I recover?" as touching upon my trust in God. To the degree that the question about recovery is valid and strong in my mind, even though it is relatively weak at present, it introduces doubt as to whether I am being ushered down the path of this journey by God. My (errant) thinking went like this: If I trust that God is totally in control, then He should heal me. Plain and simple. If I am not healing like I should, then it throws doubt onto my conviction that God is fully in control. If that were the case, then it pulls the rug out from under me. My solid trust that I will recover was based on the belief that my current illness is part of the overall plan that God has for me. If I seriously doubt that I will recover, then it undermines my belief in God's providence and His caring. So, if my question of "Will I ever recover?" is serious, then it can create a crisis in faith.

But wait a minute...Why is this a crisis in faith if I have also believed strongly that the outcome of this disease is unknown to me and I am comfortable with whatever outcome God wills? If so, the result may be that I will not recover to the point of a good outcome. So why is this question a challenge to faith? Lack of recovery may actually be totally consistent with perfect faith!

Here's why: My case seems to be different. I have already un-dergone two rounds of chemotherapy and major surgery. Overall, I have recovered well without major complications. It seems that the pivotal point in my overall outcome was the surgery itself.

Since the surgery was deemed a success, I would think that the body's recovery would follow suit and not be the point of failure. So, *I set my own expectation* for the future, whereby the body's physical recovery should proceed at the fastest rate possible until I feel back to myself. Is this expectation warranted? Let's see.

It turns out that we are now back to the point that highlights the source of the crisis and its solution. A lot of my thinking involves expectations. If those expectations are valid, then they lead to proper conclusions of my thinking and subsequent peace of mind. However, if there are expectations that are invalid, then they can lead to mismatches between those expectations and reality. Such mismatches disrupt healthy thought patterns, result in doubt, and manifest as tension, stress, pain, and anxiety. This does not allow for peace of mind and rather fosters a crisis in faith.

To reflect on today's mini-crisis, I realize that I had set up some invalid expectations.

- First, my expectation regarding the trajectory of recovery was not valid. In broad strokes, I expected that my recovery would go so smoothly that I would be able to resume normal functioning in a much shorter time than the average patient who underwent similar trauma.
- Further, I expected that there may be minor bumps in the road forward, but not major setbacks.
- Finally, I thought that God had already revealed His will by ushering me through this horrific illness until this point. By extrapolating from there, I expected that the future physical recovery was guaranteed.

Now, we can see how the mini-crisis developed. I had unknowingly made several errors in thought that led to a false set of expectations that I later felt were violated. These expectations were at two levels. On the mundane ground level upon which we live our lives, my expectations were set by empirical observations of my disease course relative to reports by other, less fortunate, patients. If I was doing well, why not expect that I would continue to do well? On the higher spiritual level, I had made an inappropriate expectation about how God runs the world. Why should I assume that His will was already revealed, and that the prior course of recovery must continue in the same way?

Indeed, the solution to my mini-crisis follows from this analysis. My false expectations required adjustment.

- First, I really do not know what my trajectory of recovery looks like. Comparison to large groups of patients from research studies or to individual patients whose stories we heard is not necessarily valid to predict my personal situation. My conditions are different, my cancer distribution was unique, my surgery was different, and so on. At best, my expectations for the course of recovery can only be general and vague. So the setback that I perceived this morning cannot be judged against any valid expectations, and therefore cannot really be judged as a serious setback. The solution to my error was to release my false expectation and to relax my thinking to allow for greater variation in recovery trajectory.

- Regarding the challenge on the spiritual level, it is entirely inappropriate and somewhat arrogant to assume what God's will looks like in the future. While it is true that nature can be relied upon to continue (i.e., we can rightly expect that the sun will rise at its predicted time tomorrow morning), and we know from ample experience that bodies heal themselves after trauma, prediction of individual outcomes is much less certain. There are plenty of unknowns, and that is where God determines our outcomes. I have no basis to expect that God will determine a fast and speedy recovery based on my perception that such happened in the past. The solution to this error was to stop assuming that "all will be OK," and rather to focus my prayers to God to ask Him to enact a complete recovery according to the speed and trajectory that He deems best.

Having gone full circle, I can conclude that my mini-crisis was based on a few inappropriate assumptions that led to false expectations, and the gap between those expectations and reality resulted in tension and pain. The correction needed was to adjust my expectations by injecting a dose of humility—not to assume that I know the natural course of my recovery and certainly not to set expectations of what God will decide for my future. The minor and temporary crisis in faith is fixed, and now the reconnection is via humility and focused prayer.

Ahh, but there is one key point that brings us home. Promise. My relationship with God is not some random connection with a mysterious Higher Power. My relationship with God has been lifelong and is based on a covenant that carries with it promises and responsibilities. I have been living that covenant and will continue to do so, with the complete trust that God will hold up His end of the deal if I hold up mine. It is not a free ride, but I have the opportunity to warrant His great rewards provided I do my part. That is a much greater topic that connects to the Torah, my role as a Jew, and what that means for my special role in this world.

FEBRUARY 16, 2019/ 11 ADAR I 5779

Ricki Pessimism for Protection?

Last night in *shul*, the *rav* was talking about change, and how we have to believe that change can happen in an instant. Even if things look a certain way, we always need to believe that it can be different and not be skeptical. I realized as he was talking that this was very comforting to me, because in some way that I hadn't even realized, I was carrying with me a certain amount of gloom and doom. I realized later that I was doing this in order to protect myself—I think I thought that if I could brace myself for the worst-case scenario, I would be prepared for anything and would only be pleasantly surprised by anything better than that.

Boy, this was a shocker for me, because I always thought of myself as an optimist, and this sure sounded as pessimistic as you could get. I realized that I actually walk around with this kind of thought more than I knew. But somehow, those words from the *rav* spoke to me now and gave me great hope. Because things can always change. That is one aspect of *bitachon*.

And I also was then able to confront this ridiculous notion of preparing myself for the worst. You can never prepare yourself, because the actual experience of the thing is *always* different than your thoughts or fears about it. And when things happen, we deal with them as they come. By imagining them beforehand, or thinking they may happen, we just cause ourselves to suffer—and for no reason! Because first of all, who are we to think we know what may happen? And second, whatever does happen can't be planned for mentally or emotionally. We just have to trust that we will be led. In addition to all of this, if we believe we are here for a reason, with a job to do, then we have to believe that we will be allowed to remain in this life for as long as we must in order to complete the job. Those are my thoughts from Shabbat. I now have a greater feeling of inner peace, and I will stop myself from thinking pessimistic—and wholly useless—thoughts.

FEBRUARY 17, 2019/ 12 ADAR I 5779

Ricki A New Level

Today we had an appointment with Professor Spitzer. While it seemed to be a good meeting, I left feeling a bit disturbed. For a while afterwards, I wasn't quite sure why. In fact, Professor Spitzer concluded that the healing from the surgery is very good. In addition, he checked Ely's vocal cords and told us that the reason Ely was having trouble speaking was because one of his vocal cords had limited movement. He did not seem too concerned, letting us know that it may resolve on its own, and if not, there are possible interventions. All in all, a good outcome. So what was bothering me? Well, he also stated that the tumor had been a very aggressive one, and that during the surgery they had had to peel it off of the carotid artery and as such, it's pretty clear to him that microscopic cells had to have been left behind. He recommended that we see the radiation oncologist as soon as possible to get things moving on that front.

This was nothing new, really. We already knew that the tumor was aggressive. And we already knew that there would be radiation because of potential microscopic cells left behind. But somehow, to me this sounded more ominous. It almost seemed as if the surgeon himself was traumatized by the rough fight that he had had with this tumor. Like a monster.

Later, after we got home, I explained to Ely what was bothering me. We talked it through, and I came to realize that this now posed a new challenge and is forcing me to give my *bitachon* muscles a strong workout.

You see, I do believe that everything is from Hashem, and that Hashem is good. But I also know that that does not guarantee that Ely will be saved from this sickness. Or does it? Well, maybe not guarantee, but I do have to believe that at the very least, he will be able to perform his mission in the world. And I also know that I need him for our tasks in the world. Really, I would like to have a guarantee—please let him live at least until Tamar is all grown up and we have had a chance to put our ideas out into the world. And maybe another twenty to thirty good years on top of that please. I do know that he was saved right now; it could have been much, much worse. And I also know that nobody has any guarantees. So I need to be thankful that he has been saved now, and believe that all of this is for a good reason. And I do know that he has so much to give to the world still. So I pray that Hashem's will is that he beats this thing completely and is allowed to go on living and contributing to Am Yisrael—and to our family in particular. And I now will raise my level of trust in God to rely on His goodness and wisdom.

Chapter 14

More Treatment?

Although we knew that after the surgery there would likely be more treatment, we had to prepare ourselves mentally for the next phase. Each phase had been so intense, with recovery periods that were really inadequate, that it was difficult to contemplate subjecting Ely's body to more of this. But of course, the goal was to eliminate the cancer, so if it meant feeling lousy for a longer period of time, then of course that was what we would have to do. On February 17 (12 Adar I), we were informed by Professor Spitzer that Ely would need radiation, which is local treatment primarily to the area of the neck which had extensive tumor growth. The next day, we met with Dr. Kursitz to hear more about the treatment plan, and she noted that the radiation would be to both sides of the neck and to the tongue. When we questioned the aggressiveness of this plan, she insisted that it was necessary. She gave us some idea of the side effects and what to expect, and scheduled a "simulation," which is a procedure in which the radiation oncologists plan out the specific parameters. She informed us that there would be a course of thirty-three radiation treatments—five days a week—and on one of the days each week, there would also be a course of chemotherapy to make the radiation treatment more effective. It was time to take a deep breath and get ready to really knock this thing out of Ely's body.

FEBRUARY 18, 2019/ 13 ADAR I 5779

Ely The Next Phase

Today marks the nineteenth day since my operation. I returned home one week ago and have been feeling generally fine, considering the circumstances. I am often reminded by my body that there is still lots of healing ahead—mild pain, fatigue, and weakness accompany me. Eating is difficult due to the need to retrain my tongue how to do its part to facilitate chewing and swallowing. Talking is strained due to slowness of the tongue and weakness of a vocal cord, and therefore I stay silent most of the time. A physical therapist is helping me build up the strength in my body, and I will be starting with speech therapy soon. In the scheme of things, the hair loss from the chemotherapy is hardly worth mentioning.

Still, I am trying to get back to familiar activities and familiar foods. All in all, I feel that I am progressing nicely on the road to physical recovery, and I am very thankful for that. I can see how Hashem is ushering me through the maze of possible health outcomes, and I feel blessed. Throughout this experience, we see many people who seem much worse off than I am, and that perspective is humbling. I can certainly attribute much of the positive results thus far to the strong emotional and spiritual support we have been receiving.[1]

Enter a new challenge—the next phase of treatment. More treatment? Yes. It is true that the operation was extremely important and was a huge success. The tumor, as we know it, has been removed. Still, as we had really known all along, the doctors are offering additional difficult treatments to attain a higher likelihood of a cure. What should we do? Haven't we had enough?

---

1   Ironically, although Ely seemed to be doing much better than a lot of people that we encountered along the way, it turned out that his survival was much shorter. You really never know what will happen, and comparing to others does not necessarily give any indication. This is another lesson that we learned toward the very end of this journey.

Professor Spitzer, the surgeon who led the operation, examined me yesterday. He feels that the healing of the surgical trauma is going well, although it will take several more weeks of recovery. He reminded Ricki and me that the tumor was very aggressive and that it had grown fast to threaten many nerves, blood vessels, and muscles in my neck. In the seven-hour surgery, he and his team carefully separated between the tumor and the normal tissues in order to remove the tumor in its entirety. He described how he had to peel the tumor away from my carotid artery—the main channel of blood supply to the left side of my brain. As a neurologist, I fully appreciate the danger of damaging the carotid; if it were to close off or were to bleed, it would cause a massive stroke. Indeed, the professor stated candidly that while they removed all the visible tumor from the carotid, it is likely that there remained cancer cells that they could not remove without damaging the carotid. In his opinion, there is no question that radiotherapy is still required. He requested that we see Dr. Kursitz, the radiation oncologist who specializes in tumors of the head and neck.

Today we met with Dr. Kursitz. She was already well-versed in my case, as she has been involved in the evaluation and planning of my oncological treatments from the start. She described the treatments that are before us, both radiation and chemotherapy. Due to the aggressive nature of the cancer, she feels it is necessary to go to all-out war on this invader. This will include thirty-three treatments (over six to seven weeks) of daily radiation to my tongue and neck, plus a once-a-week dose of a single chemotherapeutic drug. Follow-up would be with additional PET-CT diagnostic tests after three months to check for any remaining cancer activity. In her opinion, this is the standard of care, and any less would be inadequate. We asked about a newer technology called "proton beam" (touted to result in less damage to healthy tissue), and Dr. Kursitz stated that it would not be helpful due to the details of our case, including the location and the extensive area that needs treatment.

Dr. Kursitz and her nurse told us about possible side effects, including difficulty eating, skin burns, mouth sores, susceptibility to infections, and more. A scary list, to be sure, but we were reminded that all or some may not occur. Nonetheless, we were impressed that the upcoming treatment is serious business and is not going to be easy. The first step is a "simulation" of the treatment, which is the term these doctors use for constructing a detailed personal plan for the radiation based on knowledge of my case and an additional CT scan. The goal is to concentrate the radiation on the areas of greatest risk and to have the least radiation on the healthy areas. Two weeks after the simulation, sometime in mid-March, the daily treatments will begin.

The difficulty for us is both obvious and invisible. I intend to write about the invisible difficulty at another time. The obvious difficulty is dealing with the physical inconvenience of traveling to the hospital every day for over six weeks for radiation treatments, the possible pains and other symptoms of discomfort, and the predicted eating difficulty. These might seem scary, especially to people who have not been faced with such physical challenges. Indeed, I am not looking forward to more physical disability. However, the chemo and surgical treatments of the past few months have taught me that the doctors know how to manage side effects and complications. So, I am stressed about the physical suffering that may happen; but I am confident that the medical staff will take the necessary precautions and manage these in the best way.

As I am still recovering from the surgery, I am aware that the real recovery is done by the body's own healing mechanisms. The wondrous power of the body to heal itself is simply a gift from God, as built into the nature of our biology. Of course, it does not always lead to full recovery, and sometimes does not even result in survival. Much may have to do with the general state of health, strength of the body, nutritional state, and more. However, the ultimate degree of suffering and recovery is controlled by God in real time.

I have circled back to address the real question: Do the benefits of the treatment outweigh the risks of either not being treated or dealing with nasty side effects? The clear answer is YES! I must keep my grounding on this point. The goal of the entire course of treatment is to rid the dangerous cancer from my body. Doing so in the best and most expeditious way possible is my obligation. The Torah imperative of *Ve'chai Ba'hem*[2] implies that I must do all I can to survive longer to better and more faithfully fulfill my role as God's servant here on earth.

This is where prayer comes in. The prayers must be specific— focus on complete healing, minimal discomfort, and speedy recovery—all with the outlook for returning to full function with clarity of mind and a strong body. That way, I will be most fit to continue my contract with God.

As we were leaving Dr. Kursitz's office, Ricki told her that we have confidence in her. Her immediate reaction was to lift her hands upward, signaling that the true healing comes from God. We were inspired, and once again were reminded that we are being directed. We are in good hands. No need to worry.

FEBRUARY 18, 2019/ 13 ADAR I 5779

Ricki Tsunami

It's been building up, I know. But today it finally hit like a tsunami. A wave of emotion so big and so raw that it just overtook me. I cried for the life that we have lost, I cried for the pain and the trauma that we have already been through, I cried for fear of the unknown. I cried and cried and cried—big heaving sobs—feeling like our lives have fallen apart.

Earlier today, we met with Dr. Kursitz, our radiation oncologist. She told us all about the treatment plan, which is aggressive and will include weekly chemotherapy as well as daily radiation

---

2   "וחי בהם—And you shall live by them" is a verse that is understood to mean that the mitzvot should be used for living, and one should not put themselves in a position to die from them.

for almost seven weeks. She explained that this treatment is likely to have many side effects. She hit us with the fact that both the neck and the tongue will be radiated—something that we did not expect, since we were told the tongue was found to have clear margins. But apparently they are not satisfied with the 2mm margin that we had been so relieved about. When we asked her about some other treatment that we had heard about that might have fewer side effects, she proclaimed that in our case that treatment is not relevant since such a large area needs to be treated. She told us that head and neck radiation is perhaps the most difficult kind of radiation to have. The one comforting word that she used was "curative," which of course is a much better track to be on than the alternative. On the way out, I told her we are relying on them (the doctors), and she reminded me that we are relying on God.

All in all, this was an overwhelming meeting.

I was able to appreciate that very fine line that we are treading—on the one hand, the doctors have put us on a "curative" path, which includes the heroic efforts of the surgical team (as stated by Professor Spitzer), as well as aggressive treatments both before and after the surgery. (Note: Somehow the surgery all of a sudden seems like the easy part of all of this.) On the other hand, the seriousness of the situation is quite clear. We can't be complacent or have any thoughts that we have nailed this thing. So this requires us to be vigilant in our outlook, in our *tefillot*, and in controlling our thoughts. I was even able to appreciate that this thought about the fine line is a comforting one, since it is very exact and clearly orchestrated from Above. That is my point of comfort.[3]

---

3   A little explanation is warranted here. I felt that the circumstances of our story were extremely exact and precise. On the one hand, this was no minor event and there was plenty of danger. On the other hand, we were justifiably hopeful that Ely would get past this, based on the information that we had. This put us into a state wherein we had to tread this very fine line between hope and *tefillah* on the one hand, and no expectations on the other hand. The challenge here was unique, and forced us to grapple with the issues that we have written

But back to the tsunami.

You see, I can control my thoughts to a degree, but my emotions seem to have a life of their own. Despite my great efforts to align myself with the love that I know we are being showered with—both in the form of the messengers that have been sent to help us and in the form of our strong relationship which allows us to face this together—still the emotions overwhelmed me today. I have to respect that part of myself, and allow those emotions to surface from time to time. I wish I knew how to do that more gradually or more regularly.

I read an interesting blog that stated that all emotions boil down to two basic ones: fear and love. So for example, anger and sadness are really rooted in fear, while contentedness and joy are really rooted in love. I don't know what this was based on, but I found it curious that when we speak of serving God, we talk about *yirat Hashem* and *ahavat Hashem*. I haven't yet put that fact together with the speculative statement of the blogger, but maybe there's something more there that needs to be examined. In any case, it may be that the more we can latch onto love-based emotion, the less we will feel fear-based emotion. I don't know if this is true, but I can say that when I think about God as a loving parent Who has always been there for me and is familiar to me from so many positive times in my life, I feel less worried and anxious, less fearful for the future.

So maybe I just need to vent the negative emotions every once in a while, but maintain my focus on the positive things. It is still raw, and I am writing this in the middle of the night, but I am hoping that in the morning I will be able to wake up to a new day, with a bright future ahead of us.

May it be so.

---

about in this book. The reason this was comforting to me was that the very specific and exact nature of the challenge we faced was a reminder that it is from Hashem, in precisely the way that it needs to be for us.

FEBRUARY 19, 2019/ 14 ADAR I 5779

 Facing the Invisible Difficulty

After we returned home from our visit with the oncologist and the news of the day was settling in, Ricki and I felt somewhat traumatized by the apparent harshness of the upcoming treatments. Last week, I had contacted an old friend of mine who is now the chairman of the radiation oncology department of a major university in the US. He recommended that I consult with the radiation oncologists at Beilinson—the very place where we are being cared for. So, it seems that we are on the right path. Still, a series of troubling questions arose briefly in my head: Should we get a second opinion? Should we insist on a less radical treatment plan? Should I subject myself to the radiation treatment at all? How should we cope with such lingering questions?

All this indicated that I needed to look inside myself to identify and treat any insecurities. This is the invisible difficulty of this situation.

The invisible difficulty is the real culprit and represents the greatest danger to my overall well-being. As has been the case since first learning about my diagnosis, I must cope with negative forces that threaten to blacken my positive outlook. These are psychological factors that comprise thoughts of doubt, worry, anxiety, depression, and hopelessness. These are associated with stress and muscle tension. Mix into that the spiritual factors, where doubt and uncertainty try to wedge in to create cracks in my belief, trust, and devotion to God. Why do I have these insecurities and how am I coping with them?

Even though I "knew" in my rational brain that more treatment would be recommended, the imminence and seriousness of this treatment is now apparent. It is not some concept for the future but has made its way to the here and now—it is real and before us. More strikingly, these discussions with the doctors have impressed on us that the risk of the cancer is still significant; it has not been dealt a death blow—yet. Further, there is no guarantee that we will ever be able to conclude that it is "over," that the end result has been determined and there is no further risk. Rather, our treatments continue to reduce the risk. We must learn to live with uncertainty.

This uncertainty—or otherwise stated, the lack of finality about my future—can easily seed worry and anxiety about the future, as fear of the unknown leads me to paint different scenarios about what could happen. These scenarios, most of which involve what-ifs, lead to conclusions of gloom and doom. My fears of disability, side effects, and other dreaded outcomes threaten to wreak havoc unless controlled. If left unchecked, depression and hopelessness quickly follow.

As in the past, the key to my coping—to keep my negative thoughts at bay and to maintain a genuinely positive outlook—is to reexamine and reinforce my *emunah* and *bitachon*. Now, doubts about my future threaten to widen any existing cracks in my trust that God is fully in control and can be trusted. How can I cope with this situation? How can I control those annoying thoughts that pull me into worries about the future? How can I strengthen my trust in God?

The bedrock upon which my foundation of *emunah* and *bitachon* is built is the solid and unshakable knowledge that there is a Creator who established the laws of nature, created life and all its creatures, created the human race, and endowed humans with the ability to create and think. It is this same Creator who has cared for me thus far and has carried me through the maze of life, including the difficult times Ricki and I are in. He has always been in control and can be relied upon in the future.

During today's *Shacharit* prayer, I took notice of the strong lead-up to the *Amidah*. To get us in the correct frame of mind for this personal prayer to God, the organizers of the *siddur* have us repeat the great historical facts with which we are all very familiar. We purposely have no interruption between the expressions of *geulah* and *tefillah*. In the section that begins "*Ezrat Avoteinu*," we state how God took us out of Egypt, killed the first-borns of the Egyptians while sparing those of the Jews, split the Red Sea, etc. I see these historical facts not simply as a reminder of what happened long ago—the redemption from Egypt—but a promise for the future redemption. If God was there for us back then, and has been there for us ever since, then He can be relied upon in the future. On that basis, we may immediately turn to Him with intimate praise, gratitude, and personal requests. He is the only One Who can be thanked and praised, and He is the One who can be trusted to deliver the events of the future imbued with the goodness according to His perfect wisdom.

Worries and fear about the future result from uncertainty—not about the facts and rules that I would need to calculate the future but about who is in control of the future. It is no accident that we, as humans, are limited in our knowledge of how the world works to the level of detail that would be required for accurate prediction, and do not have the computational power to calculate real outcomes from the complex myriad of interacting factors. Even the most advanced physicists cannot predict the future, due to known uncertainties and complexities of nature. Such humbling realizations should only help us accept that there is a Higher Being that is responsible.

But, more on point, the challenges that Ricki and I have been facing force us to introspect, find the weak spots in our *bitachon*, and remember that only God may be relied upon to deliver salvation.

That is how I cope.

FEBRUARY 19, 2019/ 14 ADAR I 5779

Ely Caution versus Fear

Here is how I see the difference between caution and fear. It is healthy to maintain an appropriate level of caution and to take measures to ensure that I am getting the best treatment and to limit side effects. Such caution may include questions about the future, such as, "What should I expect from this treatment?" and "What are the alternatives?" Such questions about the current recommendations increase knowledge and forces the doctor to lay out the good and the bad as medical facts. Ultimately, choices about my treatment are in my control, and a healthy dialogue builds trust between the doctors and me.

Fear is quite a different animal. Fear is usually based on precious few facts and is a result of extrapolation of many possible scenarios into the future. In our situation, we are faced with uncertainty about the future and this opens many possible outcomes. If I were to use my rational brain to obsess about possible scenarios for the future, I would conclude that there is a real chance of recurrence of the cancer, long-term disabilities, and poor quality of life. The more I obsess about these outcomes, the more real they become—in my mind, they would become the likely outcomes. Worry and anxiety follow. If this were to continue, I may become hopeless about the future, even though my rational brain also tells me that I have been doing well thus far and the risks are relatively small.

So, the main difference between caution and fear is that caution relates to thinking about responsible measures that may be taken in the present based on whatever data is available, while fear relates to possibilities for the future extrapolated from little or no data about the reality of that future. To avoid fear (and all its friends), I should not obsess about what may happen in a future where the factors are unknown to me now. I do not know the true state of remaining cancer cells in my body, the ultimate success of the upcoming radiotherapy and chemotherapy in eradicating any remaining tumor, the state of my general health in the future, and many unknown factors relating to the biology of the cancer and my body's immune system in the future. I have no solid scientific basis to predict my outcome, and any look into the "crystal ball" of the future is likely to be false.

FEBRUARY 19, 2019/ 14 ADAR I 5779

Ricki Love versus Fear

Do I operate out of love or fear? This is a question I have been asking myself today. If I operate out of fear, then all of my thoughts and actions are governed by avoidance or distraction. Or perfectionism. Or the need to please.

If I operate out of love, then my thoughts and actions are governed by positivity and joy.

I know the answer to the question, and I am not happy with the realization.

Now that I think about it, I think I have always been motivated by fear rather than love. Fear that I won't live up to my capabilities. Fear that I won't be liked or loved. Fear that God will take away all of the good things in my life. Fear that some tragedy will befall me. Fear that I won't be a good enough mother. And now, this is really not serving me well. Because—add to that the fears and worries that go along with a life-threatening disease.

So how do I break out of that and start to live a life full of love? How do I focus on God and His goodness without it resulting in fear that the goodness will be taken from me? That is the work I have to do now.

FEBRUARY 20, 2019/ 15 ADAR I 5779

Ricki Living with Uncertainty

Yesterday, we met someone whose wife had been killed by a car right outside their home, just before their fiftieth anniversary. This was a tragic event that surely had major repercussions for their entire family.

How does one cope with tragedy? The answer to that question is actually not the topic of this essay. Because the answer to that question is different than the answer to my question, which is: How does one cope with uncertainty?

To be sure, there are similarities. Both require deep coping mechanisms including focusing on an overall life outlook, and most importantly, both require *bitachon*. But the concept of *bitachon* has many shades, levels, and colors, and may be applied very differently to different life situations. A tragedy such as the one described above is an event with a known outcome. The known outcome is difficult to accept and surely causes a great deal of pain and turmoil. But the resources required to overcome such a tragedy are different in nature than those required to deal with an unknown.

On the one hand, an unknown outcome has the potential to end well. There is hope. On the other hand, a person can be bombarded with worrisome thoughts about potentially bad outcomes, for which there are usually an endless number of permutations. Anything other than a completely good outcome may have bad aspects to it.

To get a little more specific and personal:

- In our situation, we don't know whether the cancer will be eradicated or not.
- If it is eradicated, we don't know if there will be lasting side effects or not.
- We don't know if it will return.
- In fact, the possible bad outcomes are much more numerous than the good outcome that we are hoping for.
- The good outcome can potentially still be followed by a bad outcome, so the uncertainty will continue regardless.

But is this any different than our usual lives? Everything is so uncertain. But we are generally unaware of all the potential dangers around us. If we were to spend our time considering all of the things that could happen, we would have no room in our brains to think about anything else. It would be an endless loop of possible doomsday scenarios. And even when things are going well, we would always have the shadow of things going badly.

So the answer can never be that only when we know that things are going well can we be relaxed and happy. It must be that we are built with the capability to be relaxed and happy *despite* all of the potential bad things that can happen. This is true both when we are not aware of the dangers, and, as in our case, when we are.

So how do we do this? Good question.

FEBRUARY 24, 2019/ 19 ADAR I 5779

Ely Gearing Up for the Next Treatments

We just returned from the hospital, where the reality of the upcoming radiation treatment settled in. Today's agenda was the simulation prior to the radiation. In order for Dr. Kursitz to deliver the best treatment, she must plan out how to focus the radiation beams to maximize the damage to the cancer and to minimize the damage to the healthy tissues. Radiation damages cells—cancer cells are more susceptible, while healthy cells have the potential to recover. Modern radiation therapy machines are programmed by computer to deliver specific doses of radiation to specific locations. In my case, since the radiation will be delivered to the head and neck, the technicians created a special mask that was molded to the shape of my head and neck, and that mask is used as a type of map that provides landmarks for the radiation machine. This planning is done based on a special CT scan performed while I wore the mask. That is what we did today.

The simulation was not pleasant, but tolerable. It lasted around twenty minutes, and then I was freed from the mask and the CT. The more meaningful part of the visit was our meeting with the oncology nurse. While we had already heard about the treatment and its possible side effects last week, the nurse we met with today explained the issues in a slightly different, and perhaps more sympathetic, way. While last week's explanation was factual and listed all the possible side effects, similar to the package insert for a drug, today's nurse was quick to mention that I may not suffer much despite the laundry list of scary side effects. Further, there are actions that I may take to prevent or minimize the troubling side effects. Today, I walked away with the feeling that this treatment is tolerable. Long, bothersome, and uncomfortable—but tolerable.

FEBRUARY 24, 2019/ 19 ADAR I 5779

Ely Possible Side Effects

Yes, there are many possible side effects to the radiation and chemo that can cause disability. But I can take two types of action to try to prevent those side effects. The first type is physical and practical, and the second type is spiritual. Here is how I understand it.

The physical actions are of two types: passive and active.

The passive measures include medication to prevent nausea, a special dental appliance to protect my teeth and jaw, a special mouthwash to prevent mouth sores, and skin cream to prevent burning. I label these as passive because these are external measures that are supposed to do some action on my behalf. For all intents and purposes, I could be sleeping, and these measures would be just as effective. They are passive—the doctors and nurses recommend them, and I must apply them to allow these chemicals and appliances to do their work.

The active type of physical action is dependent on my participation. These are primarily exercises that I may do to facilitate and hasten the body's own healing capacity. The body is endowed with the ability to heal itself in many ways that I know little about and do not understand. I am aware that some of the mechanisms are known, such as the growth of new skin cells to heal a skin wound, but a full understanding of the biological mechanisms is beyond our knowledge. To illustrate this idea of self-healing, think about this: Wouldn't it be great for our smartest inventors to include a self-healing feature in machines such as computers, automobiles, and other man-made appliances that break down? Of course, it would be great—so great that the inventor would surely become an overnight billionaire. But humans do not know enough and do not have the creative capacity to build a self-repairing computer or car. Taking this to our topic, no human has ever created an animal, and certainly not one that can heal itself.

There is precious little that we understand about self-healing, and therefore we do not know much about how to effect it. It is clear, however, that the rate and extent of healing is strongly affected by chronic medical conditions such as diabetes and heart disease, physical fitness, nutritional status, immune function, blood circulation, and various hormones and chemicals that modulate the activity of the body's cells.

What can I do to actively promote healing? After my surgery, there has been healing of muscle, nerves, blood vessels, skin, and other types of tissues that were cut, stretched, or otherwise traumatized. I have no visibility to the healing under the skin, but I am sure it is happening—seemingly without my intervention. However, anything I can do to improve my nutritional status, especially related to caloric intake and protein content, improves my healing. So, I have been carefully choosing meals and snacks that are healthy, satisfying, and rich in protein.

Further, anything I can do to improve immune function, blood flow, and hormonal balance can improve healing. For that, regular physical exercise is the key. Exercise not only improves all those factors, but also causes release of the body's internal painkillers, known as endorphins and enkephalins. Exercise, therefore, reduces pain, strengthens muscles, improves respiratory capacity, and lots more. So, while not easy, I have been engaging in regular exercise—mainly walking around the neighborhood. Today, following encouragement from Ricki, I took a quantum leap forward by attempting a short bike ride. Before my illness, I had exercised regularly, including outdoor aerobic activities (biking and jogging) and working with weights at the local fitness center. Not having done any real exercise in almost three months, I am severely out of shape. Nonetheless, I put on my sneakers, inflated the tires of my bike, and went out for a fifteen-minute ride. It went well, but I am tired, and I am sure my muscles will complain. I hope to slowly build up to an effective exercise routine (without overdoing it, of course). I have no doubt that the more exercise I can do, the better I will feel. And, I have reason to believe that my physical healing will improve. That is what I mean by active measures to promote my physical healing.

This brings us to the spiritual actions to promote healing. As with the physical actions, spiritual actions are of two types, passive and active. The passive actions relate to receiving *berachot*, while active measures concentrate on *tefillah*.

The passive type of spiritual healing action involves seeking and receiving various types of blessings that pray for and sometimes proclaim assurances of healing. Some other human being, whether a rabbi or lay person, can bless you with good health and full recovery. This is passive, since you need not do anything. Over the course of my illness, I have received many such *berachot* even though I have not sought them out. Their effects cannot be measured. When genuine caring is involved, the love and compassion conveyed in the *berachah* is helpful and supportive. Such feelings can lead me to feel more positive and hopeful, and that is certainly good.

Active spiritual measures are those that I must do myself; others cannot do them for me. Prayer is the most powerful way for me to affect my own healing. Whether in formal prayer or in spontaneous prayer, I can focus on the goodness that I receive, the Divine love that must be driving that goodness, my trust in God's powers and control of events, and the promise of future salvation and redemption. My thoughts include the well-being of the Jewish People, in general. My thoughts also include personal requests that relate to my relationship with God, my perceived mission, and requests for guidance and direction.

And, of course, my thoughts variably include crying out to God to deliver complete healing—both from the horrible disease that threatens me and from the possible adverse effects of the treatments.

- The healing that I ask for assumes that God can and will hasten my body's own physical healing mechanisms if He wills it. I ask that Hashem give me strength to do the exercises, obtain adequate nutrition, and other actions that I may do to support my body's healing.
- I ask that He grant me clarity of mind to know what is right at each step of the way.
- I know that God is responsible for the "natural" mechanisms upon which the doctors' remedies rely, and that is also a focus.
- I ask God to deliver true messengers—doctors, advisors, caregivers, and medical staff—with the necessary compassion, humility, knowledge, and skills.
- Included is my assumption that God affects the conditions and circumstances of events as He wills. These may change the disease course of a tumor, the likelihood of success of a treatment, and the likelihood of various possible side effects.

In short, while facing many challenges that are seemingly beyond my control, I am comforted by the many physical and spiritual actions that I can take to heal my wounds and to prevent future problems. That does not mean that it is easy or that I have mastered these. Far from it. My job is to learn more about the right measures to take and to do the best I can at every step. My active efforts, together with the passive treatments offered by the experts, all rely on the guiding Hand of God. So, I am trying to open that spiritual channel—the direct connection with God—through focused prayer. My experience and reason always lead me to the root cause of all, the Creator, as the only One with the power and compassion worthy of my complete trust.

FEBRUARY 24, 2019/ 19 ADAR I 5779

Ricki Wrestling with Fear

I have come to recognize the enemy. It has a name, but it does not have a face and it changes form, morphing into various shapes and colors depending on the tricks it can play at a given time. But naming the enemy is helping me wrestle with and ultimately conquer it. The enemy is *fear*.

Fear can take on a life of its own. It is often fueled by some factual information, but many times the information is partial, and may often be flawed or outright wrong. It always uses the "future axis" to do its work. And it tries to make you think it is powerful.

I have realized over the past week that fear really does have a hold on me. As much as I think I am handling the situation with *bitachon*, and as much as my intellect tells me that Hashem is with us, if I let my guard down for a second, I am consumed by fear. Last week, I really couldn't control it. Based on a few pieces of partial information, and a few of my own amateurish observations, I was practically convinced that the cancer had spread and that the prognosis for survival is abysmal. I tried to push these thoughts aside, but it just wasn't working. So two things had to happen for me to get ahold of myself. The first was that I needed to speak to a professional and to ask some questions. I was not able to reach Ely's oncologist, but we were able to speak with a friend who is also an expert in this field. Once I gave him the picture and asked my questions, my fears were allayed. It was not that my concern was unwarranted at all, and in fact, when I hung up the phone I understood that we really don't have full clarity. We are still uncertain about a lot of things, including whether the upcoming treatment will fully do the trick and whether it will cause many side effects. But somehow, I was much better able to deal with the *uncertainty* that we are living with once I put the *fear* in its place. The fear really was based on false assumptions, snap judgements, amateur interpretations, and biased observations. Once I was able to ask my questions, I was able to put all of those falsities to rest, and I was left with a much more manageable picture.

This type of thinking was in my head on Shabbat when we read *Parashat Ki Tisa*, the Torah portion in which the Sin of the Golden Calf appears. I was thinking about what made Am Yisrael forget all the miracles they had seen and succumb to an act which was seemingly irrational? In thinking about this question, I remembered a time in my life when I used to babysit for my younger sisters. I must have been about twelve or thirteen years old, and my parents would go out on Saturday nights. This was before the days of cell phones, so I had no way of reaching them. If they were delayed in returning home, I would start to panic. I would start to think that something bad must have happened to them, and as the minutes ticked by, I would peek out the window, looking and listening for signs of their car. At some point, I remember calling one of their friends at midnight in an almost complete panic. Of course, once they came home, I saw that they were fine and that they didn't even realize that I was still awake and worried about them. But during that time when the fear set in, it was possible to do very panicky things. Fear played in by leading my thoughts to a place where I was *sure* that something bad had happened. And that's where the danger of these thoughts sets in. Returning to the story of the Golden Calf, the midrash says that the people panicked because they were *sure* that Moshe was not coming back. This was based on a miscalculation or false assumption on their part. And it led to fear—and disaster.

But getting the facts rather than relying on speculation is only part of the story. The other piece, and really the key piece, of conquering fear comes back to *bitachon*. The other interesting thing in this week's reading was the *haftarah*, which tells the story of Eliyahu and his proving that Hashem is the real God, rather than the idols that the people were worshipping at the time. The interesting thing about this story is that Eliyahu tells them that they can't be in both places at the same time. They have to choose.[4] So it wasn't that they didn't believe in God at all; it was just that they also believed in other forces. They didn't put their full trust in Him and were willing to entertain the notion that other gods could also play a role. Eliyahu's message to them was—nothing doing. You can't claim belief in God if you hold onto the thought that power can come from other sources as well. In our day, these gods can be modern medicine, or other people, or even "fate," for example. So if I truly believe that Hashem is the One with all the power, then I must realize that the cancer by itself has no power. If I truly believe that Hashem is the One with all the power, then fear has no place. I realized that fear is the enemy here, and if I can confront it and not let it take hold, then I will have room in my heart for true *bitachon*. Then I won't get swayed by little setbacks or half-baked ideas or thoughts.

I had all of these ideas over Shabbat, and then on Saturday night I learned a piece by Rav Kook that Ely learned from Rav Elisha Vishlitzky, of blessed memory.[5] I didn't understand much of it, but I did get the point: He states outright that fear shows a lack of *bitachon*, and that it is at the root of idol worship. Fear must be banished in order to experience the true love and joy of God. So the take-home message is that I must conquer fear. Got it. I tossed this around in my head for a while, and at some point I went to sleep.

When I woke up today, I somehow felt much better. Much more positive. I almost felt like Yaakov when he wrestled with the angel and won. And that led me to a further thought, which I would like to explore more. Perhaps the idea of Yaakov's fight can be understood in this way: Yaakov was fighting the enemy, which is fear. He was about to meet up with his brother who, last he heard, was out to kill him. That's a pretty scary encounter. So before he could meet up with him in real life, he had to wrestle with

---

4   *Melachim I* 18:21.
5   "פחדנות", מידות הראי"ה.

the enemy. Only once he succeeded was he called "Yisrael." This is one of our unique messages as Jews in the world: *Fear and God cannot coexist in your mind.* You must overcome fear, put it in its place, before you can really let God in. I don't believe that my war with fear is over; it will probably be challenged many more times along the way. But by naming it and facing it, I believe that I have taken the first true steps to a higher level of experiencing life.

FEBRUARY 28, 2019/ 23 ADAR I 5779

Ely Can I Prevent Side Effects?

If my "work" these days is to recover from my illness, then this week was highlighted by two activities. One was the simulation needed to plan the radiation treatment. The other was a visit to a dentist to learn how to prevent side effects to my mouth.

Dr. Kursitz had recommended that I go to Dr. Adel, a dentist in Petach Tikvah who specializes in care of people with oral cancer. She explained that the radiation may cause mouth sores that can be painful and impair eating. To try to prevent that damage, Dr. Adel can make a special dental appliance, a rubber mouth guard, that I wear during the treatments. So, we followed that advice and went to see Dr. Adel. After two visits, I now have a custom-made mouth guard that is supposed to decrease the likelihood of mouth sores. I also have lots of advice for mouth care for the course of the radiation and thereafter.

During our first visit, the dentist expert in oral cancer was not in the office, so his partner and technician fashioned the mouth guard. They insisted that we return a few days later to talk to the expert. I did not want to go to the dentist the second time, since it meant more time and travel; I just wanted some down time to rest and do what I want to do before we must start daily radiation treatments next week. However, Ricki talked sense into me and prevailed. We must do all we can do to preserve health, she argued. Of course, Ricki was right. So, we went, and I was glad we did.

The real question in my mind is the role of our actions in determining whether I will be spared side effects from radiation to the mouth. Basically, can I determine if I will suffer from mouth sores? What about the natural course of disease? What about God's influence?

Here is how I think about it: Any event has causes and effects. There could be many causes, including laws of nature, the pre-existing setting, current influences under my control, conditions not under my control, and other unknown influences. It is not easy to understand how the various causes play into the ultimate outcome. Finally, it is important to understand the role of God's will. At first, all potential outcomes are possible according to the probabilities of each; once determined, only the actual outcome is experienced.

I explain below in a simplified way how this model applies to the question about preventing mouth sores, and why this thinking is helpful for me. This is just one side effect. Let's see how a seemingly simple effect results from many factors, and where I may take action.

Radiation to the mouth is an event that results in many outcomes. When it comes to the occurrence of mouth sores, we can simplify the potential outcomes to three:

- No sores
- Mild sores that cause discomfort but no functional difficulty
- Severe sores that limit eating

So, what are the root causes, and what influences may act on the system to modify the probability of occurrence of the potential outcomes? What ultimately determines if I will suffer from mouth sores?

From my limited knowledge of the general cause of mouth sores in my situation, I understand the basic damage from radiation

results from injury to the salivary glands and decreased saliva production, making it easier for bacteria to flourish. This may lead to infection of the mucosa, the lining of the mouth. A more nuanced view follows:

- **Laws of nature:** Radiation to the mouth often damages the salivary glands. Decreased saliva changes the acidity and moisture in the mouth. Bacteria stay in the mouth longer and the chemical environment is favorable for them. Therefore, there is a high chance that they can cause infection.

- **Pre-existing setting:** The known risk factors for mouth sores include poor dental hygiene, smoking or oral tobacco use, and metal fillings or crowns. Of those, I have fillings and crowns. Also, women and younger people are more prone to mouth sores for reasons that are unclear.

- **Current influences under my control:** I intend to follow recommendations of the dentist to rinse my mouth several times a day with a special rinse, use a special high-fluoride toothpaste, maintain good hydration by drinking three liters of water per day, and keep my lips moist with lip balm. In addition, I may decrease the likelihood of damage to the salivary glands by donning a custom-made rubber mouth guard during the treatments; this is recommended for people with metal fillings and crowns since the metal may disperse the radiation to the salivary glands. All these actions may significantly decrease the probability of severe sores that may impair eating.

- **Conditions not under my control:** There are many conditions that I cannot control. These include mechanical and technical issues related to the radiation treatment and its dosage, the susceptibility of my salivary glands to radiation damage, the acidity and volume of my saliva, and other factors involved in the likelihood of infections.

- **Unknown influences:** Biologists have only limited knowledge of all the factors that may influence the likelihood of developing mouth sores. There are surely more factors than the ones that I have discussed here, and those factors may interact to have significant impact on the probabilities for developing mouth sores. For example, the rate of circulation of the saliva may have an effect that is independent of the amount of saliva in the mouth, and we have no knowledge of that factor.

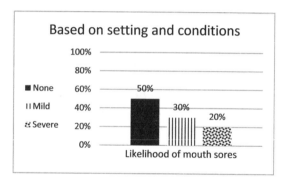

By way of illustration, this is a graph of the possibility space for this situation based on the data listed above. Obviously, I do not know the real numbers, but this representation helps me think about the likelihood of the various possibilities in an organized manner.

It seems that this is the end of the story. However, this does not account for **God's will**. Here, the system of rewards and punishments may come to bear, whereby my past merits may lead to changes in the probabilities. Also, His intention for my ultimate good may include factors that I cannot understand—and these may include the presence or absence of mouth sores that temporarily affect my ability to eat.

It is here that *tefillah* can be effective. We believe that direct appeals to God through prayer may change His will for events that have not yet occurred. One way of visualizing this effect is that the prayer may urge God to change the probabilities of the possible outcomes. In my case, prayer may ask God to decrease the likelihood of suffering from severe mouth sores. If so, prayer would help but would not determine the actual outcome. At some point, the outcome is determined. It moves from multiple potential outcomes to one actual outcome. There is no going back, as the actual outcome may be experienced by me. That event—that one instance of a possible side effect—has officially "happened."

In short, I must conclude that my own actions to prevent mouth sores may help by decreasing the likelihood of severe mouth sores but may not absolutely determine the outcome. Unknown physical factors may play a role. God's will trumps the other factors by modulating the probabilities of the potential outcomes or by some other mechanism that determines the actual outcome, and prayer has an effect.

So what can I do? It is important for me to do whatever I can to decrease the likelihood of this side effect. I can steadfastly follow the recommendations of the doctors and dentists. I can also pray to God to limit my suffering: to control the factors out of my control and those unknown to me according to His will, to facilitate my body's internal healing mechanisms, and to reduce and limit any functional difficulty that may occur.

I must remain active in this process, rather than sit back and wait to see what happens. This is a positive approach that helps me accept the outcome no matter what happens. I must do all that is in my power—to follow the recommendations of the doctors and to appeal to God in prayer. But ultimately, the outcome is not in my control.

MARCH 5, 2019/ 28 ADAR I 5779

Ricki What Is the Point of It All?

Yesterday we went for a walk in the late afternoon, close to four o'clock. We were taking a break, sitting on a bench and watching the cars and people go by—people returning home from work and school. It was a beautiful day; it had rained earlier but now the sun was out, and everything had a fresh feel. There was a slight breeze, with the sun on our backs, and it was very comfortable sitting on that park bench. It had all the ingredients of a pleasurable experience.

But for some reason, I wasn't feeling good. As we were sitting there, watching the world at that hour of the day, I was struck with the pointlessness of it all. We are born, we live for a while and we die. What are we even here for? All these people are on their way home, only to start another day tomorrow. We all have worries and anxieties and struggles. And all for what?

I think that one reason for my mood was the fact that we are about to start the next round of treatment. But it wasn't just that. I was struggling to find the source of happiness inside. I started talking to Ely about this, but since I was so negative, all it did was bring both of us down to a negative place.

This morning I woke up with a bit of insight. Here are some of my thoughts:

- We *are* here in this world. That is a fact, and no amount of wondering why will change that. Let's just sit with this fact for a minute. No matter what angle you see it from, there is no denying it. We are here. In this world. If we can take a deep breath, and accept it for whatever it is and whatever it means, then we can be calm.

- We cannot figure out why we are here or why the world was created. We have some hints of it in our tradition and through the Torah, but in reality, we are not smart or insightful enough to really understand it. Accepting this requires a level of *anavah*, because we generally think we can figure things out. Along the same lines, we cannot figure out why the world is the way it is, why we were created the way we were, why our life circumstances are such and such, or anything else having to do with our being here in the world. So what can we do? For one thing, we can try our best to follow the guidelines that we have been given, as spelled out in the Torah. This has been given to us as a gift; it is a map for living life in the way it should be. In addition, we can try to do good in the world. We can figure out our unique talents or messages, and we can do our best to put those out there. What will this do ultimately? Again, we don't know. But we don't *need* to know either.

- If we can accept that we are here, and that we can't figure it all out, we can relax. It is not our job to figure out the point of it all. Wow, that actually is a burden off of our shoulders. Think about it. That part is not our job. We don't need to be the drivers of the whole world. We should not have the world on our shoulders, because if we try to we will get crushed under the weight of it. That is God's job. It is our job to be here in our little corner of existence and to do our best with what we have been given. Only once we relax can we find both pleasure and purpose.

- That being said, I believe we are meant to search for *our* purpose. That is part of the deal. That does not mean that we should search for Ultimate Purpose. It just means that given all of the facts above (we are here in this world, with these particular circumstances, etc.), we *can* and must figure out what we do best.

- Sometimes we think too grandly. We think that we have to understand the whole world, while really we need to focus on the small things. If we concentrate, we realize that the small things are actually big and miraculous. Take birds, for example. You can find birds almost anywhere, but what is the point of the birds? The birds for me represent life in all of its variety and beauty. Birds exist, well, because they do. The birds (I assume) do not ask why. They just do what they are here to do, and in doing that, they also give us humans pleasure. They are most likely not aware of that ability at all. But they don't need to understand that in order to live their lives. They are alive, and they seem happy with that.

- I started to think about our thoughts in two directions: we can have horizontal thoughts or we can have vertical thoughts. Horizontal thoughts are thoughts that go out-ward. We try to figure out what will be the results of our actions, for example. Or we try to imagine what our lives will be in the future. These thoughts are related to the earlier question that I had about the "point" of it all. If we let our thoughts go too far in the horizontal direction, we will get stuck. It is inevitable. Because in that direction, only God knows the end of the story, and only God knows the beginning. Instead, we should train our thoughts to go in the vertical direction. Vertical thoughts are thoughts that focus more on our inner existence: What do we feel? What do we experience? What is happening in this very moment in time? What can we be doing better right now? Can we appreciate what is all around us, whether it is a relationship or a part of nature or some other element of our lives?

So my focus has started to shift, and I will try to live with these focus points more and more.

Chapter 15

Chemoradiation, Initial Weeks

On March 6 (29 Adar I), the course of chemoradiation began. We were told to show up in the ambulatory oncology ward at 7:30 a.m. for chemotherapy, and afterwards to report to the radiation department one floor below for the first radiation treatment. The nurse in the chemotherapy department, Yael, was to accompany us weekly. She was extremely kind and professional, and throughout the process we felt cared for by her and the other staff members. The chemotherapy treatment consisted of an IV infusion which took approximately three hours—including about an hour of steroid drip, an hour of the actual medication, and an hour of fluids. The radiation treatment was administered by different staff members, and lasted about ten minutes each time. Including waiting times, we generally were in the hospital on Wednesdays from about 8 a.m. to 3 p.m. On the other days of the week, we were scheduled to show up for radiation at 12:40 in the afternoon. Sometimes the wait was long (over an hour) and sometimes the wait was short (less than ten minutes), so it was difficult to predict how long it would take. During the first few weeks of treatment, Ely did not have many side effects; the dreaded mouth sores had not yet appeared, and the difficulty lay mainly in extreme fatigue overall and discomfort during the treatment sessions. In addition, the effects of the surgery were still very much apparent, including pain, inability to speak or eat much, and stiffness.

MARCH 12, 2019/ 5 ADAR II 5779

Ely I Admit That I Am Suffering. Now What?

Today I awoke with a stunning realization: I am suffering. Why is this so stunning? True, I did not think that I was suffering. But, is it that I have been suffering for a while and I just now recognized my suffering? Alternatively, is it that I was not suffering before and that now I started suffering?

Since the beginning of this journey, when I first learned that I had cancer, I have been fighting to retain a positive attitude—to the point where I quickly forget my pain and focus on the good parts of my life. Wait a minute. You'd think that it is good to keep a positive outlook, and indeed it is. But now I am aware of suffering and must find a way to get above it without denying it.

I am not prone to complaining. In several past journal entries, I referred to my symptoms as minor nuisances or annoyances. I have not thought about my overall condition as "suffering." I have stubbornly insisted on seeing the positive side. After all, there are plenty of positive aspects to my life, even considering my illness. In addition, I try not to alarm my parents and all other concerned family and friends.

But this morning I saw my current situation in the light of a series of worsening pain and difficulty. I must admit that I really am suffering in a number of ways that challenge not only my physical comfort and capabilities, but also my emotional and spiritual well-being. And I decided that expressing this is important for the sake of maintaining internal honesty and helping me overcome the experience of suffering.

Here is how I understand it. First, I see suffering as different than pain. Pain is a subjective experience that depends somewhat on the cause but mostly on how my brain perceives the physical or emotional reasons behind the pain. Clinicians commonly measure pain by using a ten-point scale, whereby the patient compares the intensity of his pain experience to the worst pain he has ever felt. There are some physiological measures of pain, such as effects on the regularity of the heartbeat and the amount of sweating, but these have poor correlation to the patient's own subjective assessment. Further, psychologists have found that the way we remember the pain is quite different than how we would rate the pain at the time it is experienced.

I am learning that suffering is much more: It is the combination of the pain perception and my attempts to deal with the pain and its emotional overtones. If I want to complain, I have a list of gripes. My neck is stiff from the trauma done during the surgery, and that limits my motion and causes pain. My voice is severely impaired, making it hard to talk and communicate in the usual sense. Singing is out of the question. Eating is difficult due to loss of appetite and tongue weakness. Each of these difficulties and pains is minor, but together, they add up to a significant amount of functional difficulty. The biggest change recently is the higher degree of fatigue and head pain, and the limits to my ability to concentrate and function in any way close to the way I am used to. For me, suffering comes down to the following distinction: Have I *reacted to the pain experience* with negative psychological symptoms, such as depressed mood, or am I determined to live a vital life *despite the pain*?

Today, I received the fifth dose of the radiation treatment. That is, five out of thirty-three. Still a long way to go. Over the past few days, I have been weak and fatigued. My level of function is so marginal that I take naps after each activity. *Shul* in the morning, then a nap. A thirty-minute walk with Ricki, then a nap. Return from radiation, then a nap. Some days, I also nap before dinner. Each nap is short, but they are frustrating signals of loss of vitality.

So, why have I now decided to consider that I am "suffering"? It is my acknowledgment that my pain and discomfort are affecting my psychological state. I find that I am frustrated and have a depressed mood much more often than I care to admit. The tipping point for me is the clear distinction between a decision to grimace in pain and lie down in bed and the more positive decision to engage in a productive activity or physical exercise. I find that over these past few days, I have a much greater tendency to go back to bed. That has a compound effect on my spiritual well-being. I may lose my grounding and sense of purpose. I may lose hope that I will get better. I may lose trust in God.

My suffering is entirely subjective. No one else can hear about my symptoms and decide whether I am suffering. In my experience as a neurologist, I have observed that many people with serious illnesses, such as Parkinson's disease, have positive attitudes and live productive lives, while others succumb to their physical limitations with depression and despair. Viktor Frankl and other mental health leaders have emphasized that each of us is in control of how we think about our pain, and whether it results in debilitating suffering. The alternative is to find the meaning in the suffering and use it as an opportunity to grow.

So, my admission—my coming out into the open—with the fact that I am suffering causes me to reevaluate how I am coping with it. More to the point, since I am feeling negative, I must get better at coping.

As I am writing this section, it is now evening time. I feel relatively good, playing Vivaldi in the background and sipping an Alexander beer. (Alexander is an Israeli boutique brewery that I patronize because they make a point of buying wheat from farmers in southern Israel who are struggling due to the economic impact of missiles and incendiary balloons.) Am I still suffering? Really, I am on the fence. I am experiencing the subjective negative expressions of suffering. And yet, I am fighting to overcome the suffering. The very act of writing is therapeutic in that respect. Overall, I feel that I caught this in time.

The point of this all, however, is not to declare that I am (or am not) suffering. It is to honestly face challenges to my emotional and spiritual well-being, to develop early detection and correction mechanisms, and to be stronger to face future challenges. I must find reliable ways to perceive my painful experiences as something other than a debilitating state that deprives me of my very essential will to live a vital life—the will to complete my role in this world. In the final analysis, I do not want to be deprived of the essence of who I am.

I am now fatigued and ready to close up for the night. To be continued...

MARCH 13, 2019/ 6 ADAR II 5779

 Suffering, Part 2

I have awoken this morning to a better mood and to some fresh insights. Having admitted to myself that I am suffering, I am now eager to readdress the matter of converting my pain into a constructive experience. But how?

True, I have dealt with this matter in a less direct way many times along my journey while coping with cancer. Each time I find strength in my trust that God is in control, He has a plan, and He is good. I find comfort in the position that I cannot possibly understand the perfect wisdom and perfect goodness of God, and therefore it is fruitless to think that I can judge Him for causing my illness. But my recent admission has caused me to face a different challenge: How can I face my suffering in an honest way, and then think about it as a "positive" experience?

If suffering is a form of mental anguish, it is entirely in in my head. **This point is key**. My suffering cannot be estimated or measured, or even declared, by anyone other than me. And the causes of the suffering are not necessarily visible. For example, one person may be suffering from the immobility of a broken leg, another from the fact that she has frequent arguments with her husband, another from the difficulty in advancing in his career, and another from the reluctance of her thirty-year-old son to get married. Each case is legitimate, and each is accompanied by anguish. There is no objective metric. The only relevant measure of suffering is the degree to which the cause results in mental anguish, which may include depression, apathy, impaired functioning, lack of energy, or other symptoms of mental stress.

My suffering is, therefore, entirely in my head, i.e., in my thoughts. Potentially, I can control it since I should be able to control my thoughts. If daily radiation treatment is causing physical weakness, I can choose to respond with frequent naps and have happy thoughts in between, or I can choose to become obsessively frustrated, depressed, and despaired from the fear that I may never feel good again. In a nutshell, that is the pivot point of the past few days. So, to allow my analysis to progress, I will reduce my current situation to that simple decision: live vitally and productively between naps or succumb to frustration and depression the entire day. Rationally speaking, I should choose the former. But our human minds are not rational—we are complete people where emotions and soul play essential roles in our lives. All three factors are critical. How then to negotiate a solution between my rational, emotional, and spiritual components to result in vitality in the face of pain and disability?

Here is my approach:

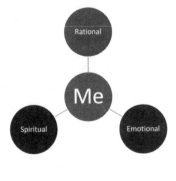

- Any experience that I have is a result of my own thoughts and the way I perceive the world. That perception is entirely personal. It is based on my senses, the way my brain has been trained to make sense of sensory information, my past experiences, my biases, and my emotional and spiritual state.
- The only conscious control I have is via my rational brain. My emotions and spiritual experiences function on a deeper level. I may become aware of emotional and spiritual thoughts, but never fully.

- The end goal is to push my emotional thinking to a positive place in a reliable manner. The mental anguish of suffering is a composite emotional state that I aim to change. This is potentially a perennial tug-of-war between the cold facts presented by my rational brain and the touchy-feely emotions. Generally, the rational brain overwhelms the soft emotions, and depression sets in.
- **The lever is my spiritual thinking**. This is the key element and the most mysterious, poorly-understood type of thinking. Whether the origin is through education, ritual, self-awareness, meditation, or Divine inspiration itself, I may only experience such thinking as it is perceived and interpreted by my rational brain.
- All three components—rational, emotional, and spiritual—are integrated to comprise my sense of self at any given moment.

For me to overcome the emotional thoughts of disability driven by the rational thoughts of physical pain and disability, I must enlist the spiritual thoughts of higher purpose and meaning of life.

Here, I must focus my rational thoughts on three major spiritual axes:

- The first axis is the abundance of good that I have in my life.
- The second axis is my relationship with God, consisting of love, faith, trust, and covenant.
- The third is the purpose of my life in this world, and the inherent promise associated with my covenant made with God.

The core of my strength in this regard comes from belief in the providence of a Higher Being—God. Jewish tradition teaches that God is the Creator Who is also in control of the world. He endowed humans with brains capable of creating and making moral decisions, and He made each individual responsible for his own thinking, actions, and moral decision-making. We are to trust that He is always caring and good, and we are to be comforted that these facts will remain for as long as the world exists. All three of these axes interact and affect one another: the trust in God and my relationship with Him, my covenant and the promise inherent in that, as well as God's goodness, and together they form an overall picture.

The personal extension of my faith is the knowledge of who I am as a unique individual in this world. I have been given gifts, talents, circumstances, and loving relationships. All for the express purpose of fulfilling my potential for whatever roles God has in store for me. Those roles include relationships, raising children, contributions to community, and work. God is One, and He has one overall plan for the world. My roles in that plan are granted to me as life progresses as a series of events. Those events may have immediate pleasure or pain, and will result in more distant consequences that are impossible for me to know.

The hardest part in all this is that our rational brains get in the way with facts and questions relating to the fact that bad things happen—for seemingly no reason. This seems to challenge the premise that God is in control or that He can be trusted to be good. This is not a sticking point for me, as I fully get the fact that I am not smart or knowledgeable enough to judge God—I do not know all His rules, and I cannot possibly compute all the consequences of events. So, I remain comfortable in my core faith.

In short, my satisfaction in life boils down to my ability to *complete my roles in life, one step at a time.* This translates to meaning and purpose in my life.

If I can remember these spiritual truths even when I experience pain and disability, then I may succeed in focusing on my purpose in life and overcoming the anguish of suffering.

MARCH 18, 2019/ 11 ADAR II 5779

Ely Daily Challenges

Today is the ninth day of radiotherapy—nine out of thirty-three. Chemotherapy once a week and radiation five times a week. People ask: How's it going? How am I doing? How is Ricki managing?

The easy part is the technical. Traveling to the hospital each day, undergoing the treatments, and the occasional visits with doctors, nurses, and dieticians takes up a lot of time and is tiring. Ricki insists on being present when I undergo chemo and when I have a doctor's appointment. We have accepted help with rides for one or two days per week, and that takes some of the load off Ricki. The radiation treatment itself is difficult due to the fact that my head is literally pinned to the table using the custom-made mask designed to prevent motion. Since the treatment itself lasts less than ten minutes (my best guess is five to six minutes), this experience is tolerable. I emerge from the radiation looking dazed, but we promptly get in the car and drive home. The technical part of this has become routine.

The harder part is the side effects. I am happy that the dreaded side effects related to mouth sores have not occurred, but I do have a host of other side effects. I have gotten used to a daily condition of waxing and waning symptoms that present steady challenges to my overall well-being. This is marked primarily by tiredness and fatigue, pain, and aversion to food.

MARCH 20, 2019/ 13 ADAR II 5779—TA'ANIT ESTHER

Ely A Purim Miracle on Ta'anit Esther

I feel that today there was a mini-reversal—a miracle of *ve'na-hafoch hu.*[1]

Just this morning, I was feeling very weak and told Ricki that I was ready to accept that my task through the end of the radiation treatment is just to survive. My physical state has been slowly deteriorating in subtle ways. Most bothersome to me is the fatigue and lack of energy to do much of anything. Add to that, mounting difficulties in eating that stem from a combination of poor appetite, difficulty swallowing, difficulty chewing, and general decreased pleasure from eating. The problem with my voice is apparently due to (partial?) damage of the nerve that activates my left vocal cord, so my verbal communication is very limited. Other lingering discomforts relate to my neck, particularly muscle stiffness and intermittent pain.

We just returned from a long day at the hospital—it was chemo day #3 (once a week, for a total of seven), and radiation day #11 (out of thirty-three). The day started poorly. I felt too weak to go to *shul*, and when I started putting on my *tefillin*, I felt a strong wave of exhaustion that caused me to sit during almost all my davening. I managed to eat a bowl of soggy Cheerios and then we headed out to the hospital. Ricki was also feeling somewhat ill due to a migraine headache. The combination of our states must have appeared appropriate for the oncology waiting room.

Then…as the intravenous medications were coming to my arm, I noticed that I had more energy. I was able to eat a few snacks that Ricki prepared (I did not fast due to my illness), and my sense of the vibrancy of myself started to improve. I noticed that my voice was stronger, and I conjecture that the weak vocal cord was active in producing some of the new low rumbling tones. This improved

---

1 ונהפוך הוא—literally: "And it was reversed." This refers to the special miracle of Purim, wherein the decree that Haman had made to kill the Jews was reversed, and he himself was hanged, along with his ten sons.

state continued through the end of the chemo and even through the radiation treatment. When it was time go home, I volunteered to drive—quite a surprising offer since Ricki has been doing all the driving and my ability to drive would have been unthinkable earlier in the day. Yet, I felt that I could do it, and Ricki readily captured the opportunity to rest during the drive. Indeed, I drove to Modiin, picked up Tamar, and all was fine.

I am now writing this piece, a feat of concentration that I have not been able to mount for over a week. Mind you, this level of functioning would be an utter failure in normal work, as I am barely able to do even the minimal things that I am describing.

So, what happened? A good question, to which I have no good answer. Indeed, a paradox arose—my small step-wise improvement occurred during the chemotherapy on a long and exhausting day of multiple treatments. There was no obvious outside cause. So the situation is all the more mysterious, and I will not have a good mechanistic explanation that could satisfy my usual desire to connect cause and effect.

Here are my thoughts: **The answer lies in the mysterious unseen factors, and not what we are able to see.**

At first, my statement may seem wildly unscientific and boorish. How could I attribute events in this world to factors that I cannot observe or measure? Have I traded in my scientific viewpoints for magic, voodoo, and the occult?! *Of course not*, as I will explain briefly.

Science itself, while amassing impressive successes in discovering how parts of nature work, is admittedly lacking in a complete understanding of matter, energy, biology, and all other fields of study. In fact, the more we discover, the more we realize how poor is our understanding and how much more still needs to be discovered. In my own field, many principles have been worked out regarding the workings of brain cells and brain circuits, but scientists have no real handle on the major questions relating to human function, thoughts, subconscious, and consciousness itself.

Science is based on observation and experimentation. What you see can be the basis of a theory or a physical law, but there is so much that science cannot or does not measure, that it is doubtful if it can possibly address the greater questions of mind, body, and soul. In the case of today's experience, science cannot provide a satisfactory answer, since the entire phenomenon is based on my physical feelings, and ultimately my overall assessment of well-being (a personal sense that is not well-defined or quantifiable). These are not observable to an experimenter or measurable by any instrument.

In quite a rational train of thought, I have used my *personal experience* as the strongest evidence of the phenomenon that I described above regarding the "quantum jump" in my well-being today. Personal experience should not be ignored nor diluted by forcing it to conform to the theories or personal thoughts of other people, even eminent scientists, philosophers, or theologians. The truer my memory is to my real experience, the better my possible understanding of what happened and how it happened. I offhand reject any thoughts that my experience occurred as a random or lucky event, as the chances of this happening are not plausible.

The best I can guess is that some non-physical cause affected me. That cause could have been internal to my mind or external to my mind.

- **Internal causes**, such as positive emotions of gladness, relief, or relaxation are possible explanations for a major change in mood and well-being. These emotions and feelings are presumably special types of thoughts that are mediated by complex brain circuits in the brain. It is possible that the thoughts are internally generated and are triggered by our sensations of the external environment, including vision, hearing, touch, and taste.
- **External causes** are those that come from outside us—from the good energies of other people or from some

other hidden source of positive energy. True, the chain of thoughts from external causes may lead to positive emotions and assessment of well-being, but the root cause is external, and not internal. These external causes are of the nature that it is very hard to clearly identify the source. Sometimes, a personality such as a loving parent may be influential by imparting a strong dose of love that can tip the balance to positive thinking, but generally, more subtle influences may be present and difficult to sort out. Hidden sources of energy are non-human and mysterious—these are the most difficult to appreciate and understand. Beliefs play a major role. Judaism teaches that such hidden causes in our lives are manifestations of God's Divine providence, *hashgachah pratit*, and reflect His will in controlling world events at the individual and collective levels. The energies are related to Divine love, caring, goodness, and perfection.

Thinking back to earlier today, my memory does not provide support for the idea that sensory stimuli alone triggered my change in feelings. This change was noticed by me over the course of around sixty to ninety minutes, while sitting quietly in the oncology treatment booth with Ricki. We were not visited by a medical clown, nor was there any identifiable happening that could be thought of as "happy." Further, I do not recall thinking happy thoughts related to this period. Therefore, I do not accept that internal causes, if present, were significant in today's change of state.

Regarding the possibility that external personalities were significant in effecting my change in feeling, there were no other people involved (there were two oncology nurses who were very efficient and business-like, not touchy-feely). Other patients were generally sad-looking and sickly, and there was no particular Purim happiness in the area. So external people are not the explanation.

I must conclude that an external non-physical, non-human, spiritual energy was the cause. Since my Jewish belief system is based on the fundamentals of *Shema Yisrael Hashem Elokeinu Hashem Echad*[2]—the truth of the Oneness of God and His providence in the world—the general explanation is apparent. God is the *only* Ultimate Source (my favorite source of thinking on this is the first chapter of *Chovot Halevavot*, written in the eleventh century by Rabbeinu Bahya Ibn Paquda). God's Divine love, while inconceivable to us, powers the entire physical world; and His constant goodness and direction characterize His unique providence. As such, there is no other candidate.

Based on my conclusion, I may conjecture that today's unexpected change in state was due to God's plan for my well-being during this illness. He continues to place before me new challenges that force me to choose how to think about my physical suffering and the set of facts presented to me; essentially, I am challenged regularly to cope with my life situation. On a daily and hourly basis, I may decide to succumb to fatigue and discomfort and lie in bed like a sickly person, or instead to exert special effort to eat, exercise, and do some degree of productive work. I may reassess my values, my worldview, and the strength of my belief.

Realizing these challenges, one response is to cling closer to my trust in God, and to pray strongly for Him to help me and guide me through these challenges. I may realize any effects via my emotions, feelings, and sense of well-being.

I will never know God's true will and I will never know the reasons for my disease or the ups and downs of my daily physical condition. But I do know the big picture of Who created the world and Who runs the world. I thank God for feeling better today and pray that it continues. Maybe this is a hidden miracle for Purim…

---

2   שמע ישראל ה' אלוקינו ה' אחד—Hear O Israel: God is our God, God is One.

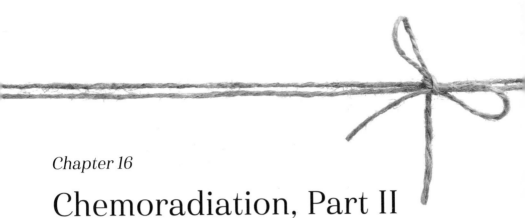

Chapter 16

Chemoradiation, Part II

After the first half of chemoradiation, things started getting worse. Ely started getting painful sores in his mouth, which prevented him from eating and made it difficult to even drink the shakes prescribed by the doctor. He started taking more pain medication, and it was a fight to finish the treatments and to maintain nutrition.

APRIL 1, 2019/ 25 ADAR II 5779

Ely The Halfway Milestone

Yesterday we reached a milestone. I received the seventeenth out of thirty-three radiation treatments—past the halfway point. Why is this so encouraging? Because it means that we can do this. It has been hard and may get harder. So arriving at the halfway mark gives us new strength. But—that does not make it easy.

As much as we would like, we cannot escape reality. We have learned that radiation therapy to the head and neck is no laughing matter. This treatment focuses strong X-rays onto the places where any remaining tumor is suspected. Unfortunately, in addition to harming the tumor, it also harms the healthy tissue in the surrounding areas, including my neck, my tongue, and my mouth. Inflammation in the neck is causing pressure on the nerve that controls my vocal cord, and so my voice is no louder than a whisper. Damage to my tongue has caused painful sores.

The good news is that the healthy tissue is supposed to heal, although that will take some time after we finish the course of radiation. In the meantime, I am living with some of the expected side effects, including burns on my skin, sores on my tongue, fatigue, and general lack of energy. The greatest challenge is the daily fight to eat enough food to provide much-needed calories and protein. For that, the dietitian has recommended specific foods and nutritional supplements.

From a practical point of view, we have shifted to a different mode. With guidance from the doctors and nurses, my activities for the remaining time of the treatment are no longer aimed at normal function. Rather, they are highly focused on "simply" getting through the remaining few weeks of the treatment. I have been told to take more pain medications so that I could eat more without worrying as much about mouth pain. In addition, I have been given medications to help heal the tongue. Regarding nutrition, the normal idea of eating plenty of fruits and vegetables is out the window. Rather, I must use whatever energy I have to eat soft foods that are rich in protein and calories. Since I cannot get enough from normal foods, Ensure nutritional shakes have been prescribed. While packed with all the necessary nutrients and vitamins, these are not the panacea, as I have found it difficult to stomach them.

Just going to the treatments and the related doctors' visits, preparing and slowly eating the calorie-rich foods, and resting when needed literally takes up the entire day for both Ricki and me. I have not been to *shul* in several weeks, as that tires me out. It is easy to get discouraged by my current physical condition.

The bright side is that all the doctors and nurses keep telling us that I will return to normal function. We just have to wait until the treatment finishes and then can start the recovery process. The ENT doctors say that my voice should improve, and they have recommended a talented speech therapist to help. My appetite should return, and my weight should be restored. All the sores and tissue damage should heal. It will just take time.

This half-way milestone has great psychological benefit. It is reassuring to know that we made it this far.

APRIL 2, 2019/ 26 ADAR II 5779

Ricki Resentment toward Whom?

I remember that when we first found out about the cancer, a few people mentioned the word "anger" or "resentment." Some people told me that if I just want to "vent," they would be there for me. Or if I want to punch the wall, or in some other way express my anger at being faced with this situation, it would be perfectly acceptable and understandable. I remember thinking: *I don't understand that at all.*

- For one, I am not prone to anger, and in fact have more of a tendency to let things go even in circumstances when anger is the appropriate response.
- But more than that, I remember thinking: *Anger? I don't get it. Who would I be angry with? God?*

Now we are at a point that we have been at this for almost half a year, and the treatments right now are very intense. Ely does not feel well, tires easily, and needs my help with trips to the hospital and doctors, filling of prescriptions, trying to find foods that are edible for him, and other tasks. On top of that, Pesach (Passover) is coming, which always adds a layer of stress to my life. And it just so happens that during this time period, there have been a few other events that have required my attention, including a minor surgery for one of my children with an overnight hospital stay, and a minor but irritating legal issue.

Yesterday, I realized that I reacted uncharacteristically in anger when someone was blocking my driveway. Often, people drop off or pick up their kids right next to the driveway of our building, since there is a school nearby and no parking on the street. There are, of course, other solutions, including going around the back street where there is parking, or pulling up farther down the street. But out of convenience, parents often choose to pull up right near what happens to be our driveway, sometimes also blocking it from cars going in and out. While I generally find this annoying and inconsiderate, I don't usually respond with anger when someone does this. But yesterday, a woman was completely blocking the driveway when I wanted to leave, and she was waiting for several kids to pile into her car, which was taking longer than it needed to. I honked a few times, and then I honked again, loudly and held it down for a few seconds to make my point. When she looked over at me apologetically, I responded by lifting my arms in a gesture of "What are you doing?" She then quickly closed the back door and drove off, almost certainly without making sure the kids were safely buckled. After this incident, I realized that I had to calm down. Why should her "lack of consideration" make me react that way? Even if she was wrong in blocking my driveway, I didn't have to get emotional about it! I surprised myself with my reaction, and the disappointment in myself stayed with me until I got home and told Ely about it.

Today, I realized why I had reacted that way. I was feeling overwhelmed with everything that was going on, and I was starting to feel, yes, resentment, about my life and the number of things that keep piling on top of what is already a difficult situation. And when I started to think about it, I realized that the resentment could be only one thing—anger at God. It is hard to admit, because I really do not think I have any right to be angry with God. Moreover, I believe that everything that God has given me and continues to put into my life is good—either explicitly (wonderful children, enough money, supportive family, etc.) or in a more hidden way (i.e., all of the challenges that I have to face, which ultimately will be for my own benefit, whether I see it now or not).

Yesterday morning, I went to the Kotel to welcome my son Eitan home from Poland. Their group was supposed to arrive at the Kotel at 5:45 a.m., so I made sure to get there on time. After the initial hugs and some time to get reacquainted with our children, we had *tefillah*, followed by some refreshments and then a ceremony. Suddenly, before I knew that the ceremony was coming to an end, they started to sing. It was at that moment that I became emotional. I was thinking about how the Jewish People went through such a difficult *galut*, with tremendous pain and suffering along the way, but all along maintaining their *tikvah*, their hope, for redemption. There we were, standing with the Kotel and Har Habayit in the background, with a group of young men, including my own son—a scene which would have been unimaginable not so long ago—singing about hope. Singing *"Ani Ma'amin"*—I believe. And it all became one story for me, as I was standing there singing, with tears in my eyes and falling down my cheeks. Yes, we sometimes have pain and suffering. But there is a bigger story here. There is hope and there is belief that Hashem is leading us to something that we can't even imagine.

So where is the place for anger or resentment?

It is good that I recognized it, that I felt it, and that I can now put it in its place, which is outside of my head. There is no room for anger when you take a step back and look at the bigger picture. And while I am still a bit overwhelmed with everything that I need to deal with right now, without the overlay of resentment, I feel that it is all manageable. Hashem will get us through this difficult time, and God willing we will emerge to see a new reality on the ground—one which is currently hard to imagine, but which undoubtedly includes a closer connection to and belief in God than what was previously there. *Ani ma'amin.*

APRIL 3, 2019/ 27 ADAR II 5779

Ricki Hard on Myself

"Don't be hard on yourself." Those were the words that Ely said to me this morning. You see, I was starting to feel like I can't trust my decisions, because of a few relatively minor decisions I had made over the last day or so. And I was having a hard time connecting during *tefillah*. So I started to feel like there's something that I should be "getting" but that I'm not. My general feeling this morning was no longer anger or resentment; rather, I was feeling puzzled. I sort of felt bewildered, sitting in the waiting room waiting for the nurse to call us in for chemotherapy. How did we get here? Why are we in this room? What is really going on?

Even though we have been coming here regularly, nearly every day, today it felt strange. So what am I missing?

Well, for one thing, I have to not be hard on myself. I have to know that I am doing my best in a very difficult circumstance, and that maybe the clarity will only come later.

What I do need to work on, though, is my connection to Hashem. I need to cry out for help every day, and to ask for salvation. Maybe that is what I am missing. But most likely, in order to do that, I need to stop being hard on myself. To relax, and to let it come naturally.

APRIL 7, 2019/ 2 NISAN 5779

Ely   Full-Court Press

It is time for a full-court press. Today I completed treatment 22/33. Just over two weeks remaining. But the difficulties are increasing, possibly threatening my ability to complete the course of treatment.

For those less familiar with basketball strategy, a few words of explanation are in order. When a team has fallen behind, the coach may call for a full-court press. That means that rather than starting your defense when the opposing team reaches your side of the court, you start your defense in the opponent's side. That type of pressure can confuse the other team and cause turn-overs. After a few minutes of such pressure, the tide of the game can change, and your team can possibly continue to victory. Of course, a full-court press takes a lot of focus and energy and therefore cannot be sustained for a long time. The hope is that it can disrupt the opponent's momentum enough that you can then go back to a more comfortable pace.

The past week has been particularly difficult. Due to the side effects from the radiation, I have not managed to eat much. As a result, I feel weak and have lost too much weight. The real problem is not the loss of a few kilograms, since I have been told that the weight will come back once I recover. The problem is that it may take weeks for me to regain my ability to eat after the treatments finish. So if we don't manage to improve this situation, I am risking an extended period of poor nutrition that could pose a serious health hazard.

The most important action that we took today was to insist on an appointment with the nurse. The radiation oncology nurses regularly follow up with all the patients to help manage the side effects. They are experts. Sure enough, the nurse immediately understood the problem, verified the weight loss, and quickly drew up a comprehensive plan. She consulted with the doctors, prepared the paperwork, and explained to us in clear terms the necessary steps to take.

In short, the nurse explained what it will take for me to eat better—improved pain control and stronger treatment for nausea. We left with a few prescriptions and a tube of ointment. More importantly, we have a detailed plan: when to take each treatment, in what order, and when is the best time to eat in relation to the medications.

There is even a fallback plan. If I will still not manage to get enough nutrition, then the plan is to insert a small feeding tube like the one I had following the surgery. If necessary, that would bypass my mouth and ensure adequate nutrition gets to the stomach. This would necessitate a hospital admission of several days. At first, I was put off by the idea of a feeding tube. But, as a worst-case scenario, this offers a real solution. These doctors and nurses have plenty of experience with my situation and exude confidence in being able to complete the cancer treatment while keeping me healthy.

As in basketball, the key element of this medical full-court press is to change the psychology of my situation from one of despair to one of hope. With the intense strategy that I have been given, I now feel that the remaining two weeks are doable. Ricki's help has been immeasurable, and her tenacity in obtaining the medications and organizing my day to make it work according to plan has been critical. Her positivity and trust in Hashem lifts me.

My job now is to focus on following the medical treatment plan and preparing for Pesach. I am literally cleaning my mouth from *chametz*. I am trying, as well, to clean my soul from *chametz*. This is truly the hard work that must be done.

I pray to Hashem to show me the way—to help direct my thoughts to the internal sources of arrogance that may be hiding in the cracks and crevices of my mind. True freedom will not come from a radiation machine. It will come from detaching myself from dependence of my self-image on thoughts of entitlement, superiority, and comparison to others. My self-worth comes from the fact that I was created by God in His image. Since the same can be stated for all other people, we are all equals. My personal mission in the World is driven by the will of God—the gifts and talents He has given me, the opportunities He provides, the health He has bestowed, and the years that He allocates. He rewards me with loving relationships and a pleasant life.

I am happy with my life and pray that I return to health soon to be able to resume my mission. If it takes a full-court press, so be it. Thank God, I have the benefit of an expert and caring medical team. Thank God, I have Ricki, my parents, my children, my brother, and many close relatives and friends. Thank God for the love He rains!

APRIL 10, 2019/ 5 NISAN 5779

Ely Appreciating God's Hand

As a quick follow-up to the full-court press, I have good news. It seems to be working. This is the third day on the aggressive treatment plan to improve my ability to eat through better pain and nausea control. Indeed, I have managed to eat foods with the required calories and protein. I have not lost more weight since then and feel much better overall. So, the plan going forward is to keep up the full-court press until no longer necessary.

Today, I received the twenty-fourth radiation (out of thirty-three) and the sixth chemo (out of seven). We also met with the dietitian. Yes, a busy day—and a happy day. All agreed that I am doing much better than on Sunday. All agreed that I should continue with the plan rather than opting for the fallback plan of a feeding tube. To be sure, this is not easy and demands much work just to make sure I take all the medications, ointments, and rinses at the right times during the day and in relation to meals. Still, Ricki and I prefer this if it will allow us to finish the treatments and to recover back to full health.

Now for the story behind the story. When we showed the aggressive plan to Malki, the dietitian, she immediately recognized the work of Sara, the nurse who helped us on Sunday. Sara composed the plan and had exuded confidence that it should work, thereby avoiding the hospital admission and feeding tube. Malki indicated that Sara is the best at this. After the radiation treatment, we stopped by the nurses to report on progress, and we were told that Sara was not there. A different nurse met with us and seemed surprised by the breadth of the treatments recommended by Sara, indicating that she would have been much more conservative. As a physician, my own tendency is to err on the side of less, rather than more, when treating pain. However, it is obvious now that (as a patient), the best treatment for me at this point in time is more aggressive pain control (at least for the short-term).

So, how did this reality come to be? Thinking back to the events of Sunday, it is clear to Ricki and me that there were many details that happened to occur in the right way and with the right timing. To set the stage properly, I need to first review what led us to this point of crisis. Early last week, I had been managing pain by taking one strong medication in an inconsistent way—only taking it as needed. Starting Thursday, severe nausea developed, and I attributed it to the narcotic pain medication. Realizing that the nausea was preventing me from eating, I went back to the weaker non-narcotic pain medicine. I took a pill for nausea, but the nausea continued and severely limited my ability to relate to food. Also, my tongue became more pain-sensitive to some flavors or chemicals in the Ensure shakes and the other foods that I tried. As a result, I ate very little for three days, during which time, I lost weight, got weaker, and felt sickly.

Here is where it gets interesting…Ricki and I went to the hospital on Sunday for the usual radiation treatment and insisted on seeing the nurse as well. While in the waiting room, Dr. Kursitz, my oncologist, passed right by where we were sitting and asked how I was doing. My report was to the point—not well. After hearing the details, Dr. Kursitz said the time had come for the feeding tube.

When we were called to see the nurse, it happened to be Sara, who I think is the head nurse. Dr. Kursitz had already talked to her about our encounter. Sara asked many questions about my condition, my symptoms, and the actual foods and medications I had managed to take. She asked that I step on the scale, and indeed there was a large drop of three kilograms during those days. Certainly, this was a crisis that deserved immediate attention. Sara then outlined her plan, called Dr. Kursitz to confirm her agreement, and asked a junior physician nearby to review the plan and sign the paperwork.

Sara was not ready to give up so easily and send me for a feeding tube. Her plan includes more pain medications, nausea remedies, corticosteroids, mouth rinses, and tongue ointments, some of which I was already taking and many of which needed to be added. The most important element, however, is the structure of the plan. Sara told us exactly when and how to take each item and wrote this clearly in a note for us to take home.

Frankly, Ricki and I were skeptical and insisted that we also maintain the fallback plan of a feeding tube in case these heroics did not work. Happily, we have found that Sara's plan is working. We are highly motivated to continue it as long as needed. If successful, it would be a major victory: I would be able to complete the course of treatment (to eradicate the cancer) and would not require hospitalization or a feeding tube.

As soon as Ricki and I put all the pieces together, we saw how **serendipitous** it was that we ended up with Sara's plan.

- Had Dr. Kursitz not **happened** to *walk right in front of us* in the waiting room, we would likely not have gotten the attention that we did. The doctor spoke to Sara before we saw her and primed her for my crisis.
- Had we **happened** to see *any nurse rather than Sara* on Sunday, we would have left with a very different plan.
  - Had Sara not been the best person for this crisis, the plan would not be as effective.
  - Had she not quickly gotten the backing of Dr. Kursitz and the execution of the junior doctor, the plan may not have been executable.
- If Ricki **happened** to have difficulty on *Sunday* obtaining the new medications from the pharmacies (in fact, she went to two different pharmacies to get everything, and it wasn't clear that she would succeed), we would have had less time to try them and may not have felt confident by today that Sara's plan is working.

In short, several key factors that were out of our control had to happen at the right time. We were not even aware of the importance of these factors and only saw how critical they were several days later. Such convergence of events to lead to what I consider a major victory was really quite improbable and beyond our control. It is not mere "luck" or random chance. This event can be viewed as a form of miracle—certainly a display of God's loving Hand.

Appreciating God's Hand at work in this very personal experiential way is inspirational and gives Ricki and me great strength. It is a sure reminder of the real way the world works—through the undetectable hidden guidance of events by the Supreme Being. Occasionally, we may glimpse hints of the great orchestration behind these seemingly random coincidences. An orchestra does not play beautiful music through random sounds from each instrument; it depends highly on the organized structure of the musical score and the skills of the conductor to manage its execution. We appreciate through insights like we had today that the world is orchestrated in a beautiful way as well.

This is *hashgachah pratit*, Divine providence in the realm of personal experience. The more I see it, the more I am lifted by it. I pray that Hashem continues providing His loving guidance to us all.

APRIL 16, 2019/ 11 NISAN 5779

Ely The Home Stretch

Only five more to go! *B'ezrat Hashem*, tomorrow will be the final chemo treatment and the twenty-ninth radiation treatment. Ricki and I are facing each day, one at a time. We are determined to complete this treatment. It seems to us that we need to gather all our strength to accomplish that—and we will!

APRIL 21, 2019/ 16 NISAN 5779—CHOL HAMOED PESACH

Ely A Seder without Matzah

For this year's Pesach Seder, Ricki and I were fortunate to have a number of our children—Avishai, Zaky, Eitan, Renani, Meira, Yoav, and Tamar—as well as my parents join us to celebrate. Months ago, when we were planning our invitations, the idea of having so many people seemed daunting.

First, we did not know what state I would be in, as we were told repeatedly that my fatigue and other side effects would be at their worst just around that time. Second, and perhaps more critical to the success of our plan, the heavy burden of cleaning and preparing for the *chag* rested completely on Ricki's shoulders. How could we increase that load?

Despite these rational reasons and other excuses, after just a few minutes of discussion, we decided that the right thing is to celebrate the *chag* with our family. After realizing that my needs would include being in my own home close to my bed, medication supply, and special shakes, we concluded that it would be best for us to host. Ricki insisted on taking on the logistical challenges and agreed to accept help where practical to do so. I insisted on hosting a relatively large group when I knew I may not be able to even sit at the table. To do so, I had to agree "to leave the table when I feel I have had enough" and "to try to do the best I can without overdoing it." With that, we would be able to turn this Pesach into a meaningful and enjoyable *chag*.

OK. Now came the questions relating to the strange situation in which I have found myself at this point in time. Even a small child knows that Pesach is the time for us to eat matzah and to drink four cups of wine.

Yet, I can do neither.

The combined treatment side effects from the chemotherapy and radiation therapy have caused several painful ulcerations on my tongue. As a result, my diet has been restricted to soft or liquid foods that do not contain chemicals or spices that may irritate the ulcers. In practice, we have found that plain-flavored or vanilla-flavored shakes made with special formulations rich in calories, protein, and vitamins work well for me. With that restricted diet, I have managed to eat enough and maintain my weight.

While discussing this with my rabbi, Rav Eli Reif of Modiin, it became clear that I would not be able to satisfy the mitzvah of eating matzah on the evening of the Seder. I strictly avoid any foods that may irritate the sores on my tongue. I told the *rav* that any form of matzah, whether the soft pita-like matzah that is now available or matzah softened by soaking in water, is out of the question. I would also not be able to drink wine or grape juice, since these would irritate the open sores due to the chemicals in these beverages. So, it seems that I have a real problem.

Then came the unexpected. The *rav* sent me a message—based on similar prayers composed when people were prevented from fulfilling a mitzvah due to conditions beyond their control, he had composed the following *tefillah*.

(*Translated from the Hebrew*) Father in Heaven, it is known to You that it is my wish to do Your will, and to fulfill Your commandments, wherein You commanded us to eat Matzah, but I am unable to fulfill this commandment this year. I am ready and willing to fulfill the mitzvah of "to live by them (the mitzvot)—and not to die by them." May it be Your will that the telling of the story of *Yetziat Mitzrayim*—as that is also a mitzvah done with the mouth—is considered by You to be equivalent to the mitzvah of eating matzah. And please allow me to live and make me worthy of fulfilling Your laws and serving You with a full heart, with strong health, in the coming years. Amen, and may it be Your Will.[1]

---

1   אבינו שבשמים, גלוי וידוע לפניך שרצוני לעשות רצונך ולקיים מצותך שצותנו לאכול מצה, אך אנוס אני ואיני יכול בשנה זו לקיימה, והנני מוכן ומזומן לקיים מצות "וחי בהם—ולא שימות בהם", ויהי רצון שתהא מצות סיפור יציאת מצרים, שאף היא מצוה שבפה, שקולה לפניך כאילו קיימתי גם מצות אכילת מצה, ותחייני ותקיימני ותזכני לשמור חוקיך ולעבדך בלבב שלם בבריאות איתנה לשנים הבאות, אמן וכן יהי רצון.

APRIL 23, 2019/ 18 NISAN 5779—CHOL HAMOED PESACH

Ely Last Zap

Note by Ricki: The last day of treatment was on the fourth day of Pesach. Ely was going to write something that day, but he was weak and tired.

Chapter 17

Post-Radiation Recovery— or So We Thought

We were told that there would be a period of recovery that at first would be even harder than the last few weeks, so we weren't too worried when Ely wasn't feeling well and wasn't able to eat.

APRIL 25, 2019/ 20 NISAN 5779—CHOL HAMOED PESACH

Ely Our Greatest Challenge Yet

We made it to the end of the radiation. A long haul it was—seven weeks of traveling to the hospital to receive a highly precise and focused schedule of radiation beams targeting the locations on my tongue and neck suspected of harboring microscopic areas of cancer cells that may have eluded the prior chemotherapy and surgical treatments. To increase the chances of success of the radiation, the oncologists decided to add a weekly dose of a chemotherapeutic drug. All told, these past seven weeks were difficult, both physically and psychologically.

Two days ago, on the final day of the radiation treatment, Sara, the head nurse, systematically reviewed all aspects of the treatment, the status of all the side effects, and current remedies. She then explained what to expect in the coming weeks and recommended additional medications that may help. She told us she would call during the next day or two to check in and asked that we come to see her in one week.

So what are we to expect? First, we were told that the physical difficulties may get worse before getting better, and I should not expect to feel any improvement for around two weeks. We were instructed on how to increase the dosages of the pain medications if needed. It will be a long and gradual process of healing. When the pain starts to subside, I will gradually decrease the medications.

You may think that Ricki and I are now breathing sighs of relief and starting to plan a vacation, or the first steps to get back to "normal" life. In fact, we have found that

Note by Ricki: This entry ended in the middle. After this, Ely was really not feeling well and was not able to write. The struggles to eat and to just maintain enough energy to get through the day were debilitating and did not allow for real work or introspection.

On May 7, 2019 (2 Iyar 5779), we had an appointment to be admitted to the hospital for a feeding tube. The "full-court press" was no longer working, and Ely's struggle to eat became an impossible task. His calorie intake went from 2,000 calories per day while he was able to drink the shakes, to 800 calories a day for a few days, and then plummeted to almost nothing. We started to be happy when he managed to eat 200–300 calories. It seemed to be a vicious cycle, where the less he ate, the less he wanted to eat. It got to a point where we realized there was no choice, and a plan was put in place to have a feeding tube inserted at the hospital.

Like with all plans, we are not really in control. The day before we were scheduled to go to the hospital, on May 6, 2019 (1 Iyar 5779), Ely was feeling extremely unwell, and we decided to go to the oncology emergency room to get checked out. Initially when we arrived, we were told that he would be given IV fluids to prop him up a bit, and then he would be sent home for the night. We were to return in the morning as planned. However, after seeing results of the bloodwork, the doctors informed us that he could not go home as planned. They needed to stabilize his electrolytes, and he would have to be admitted. In addition, they would start the feeding tube the following day.

MAY 10, 2019/ 5 IYAR 5779

Ricki Three Spoonfuls of Applesauce

Everything has changed. Let me start by saying that I just got very emotional over three spoonfuls of applesauce. The things I have started to be thankful for and to pray for have changed drastically over the last few weeks, and particularly over the last few days. Ely hasn't been able to eat for almost three weeks, and before that, eating was a chore that he was able to accomplish, but only with a great deal of pain medication. It certainly had no enjoyment. This has been going on for a long time. The last time I remember him enjoying food at all was at the Purim *seudah*. So almost two months have gone by. The amazing thing about these three spoonfuls of applesauce is that *he actually enjoyed them.* There was pleasure on his face as he tasted and felt the food in his mouth. I was crying with thanks for this small pleasure.

Description of what happened next: The next days were a blur. It became clear over the course of these days that, in fact, Ely might not be saved from the cancer. Ely and I had a discussion about this at one point. Since he had earlier expressed the very clear belief that if he did what he had to do in this world, Hashem would save him, the new situation necessitated addressing this point. He said to me, "It could be I was wrong. Or it could be that I was meant to think that way so that I would do what I had to do during this time—that is, to write this book. But really, we'll never know."[1]

---

1   This to me was a further cementing of the very high level of *bitachon* that Ely had. Even

The doctors informed us that they would do a CT scan on Monday, May 13 (8 Iyar), to check the status of the cancer. In the meantime, on Sunday May 12 (7 Iyar), Ely started to have trouble breathing. He was given oxygen to help him breathe, and we were told that they would be checking to see if there was an infection in the lungs. On Monday, the CT scan showed that the lungs were full of fluid, and it was not clear if this was due to an infection or spread of the cancer, or both.

However, the CT scan also showed that the cancer had indeed spread. Dr. Kursitz informed us that there may be additional treatments available, but that we had an acute breathing problem that needed immediate attention. Any talk of future treatment was put off until the current situation could be stabilized.

On Monday night, a procedure was performed to remove as much of the fluid as possible, both for relief and for testing. Antibiotics were administered as well. His breathing did not significantly improve.

On Tuesday, May 14 (9 Iyar), the oncologist and social worker called us in for a family meeting. Ely's parents were there as well as some of his children. In that shocking meeting, we were informed that there was a possibility that his breathing would get more difficult. We were told that if he did not improve within the next few hours, they were concerned that he would have more trouble, and if so, he would require medications that would sedate him somewhat. We were informed that this could be the beginning of the end. They recommended that we bring the important family members to see him in case he started having additional trouble during the night.

That meeting was one of disbelief and tears. We had no idea that his condition was so critical, and that things had deteriorated so significantly. True, he was weak and was on oxygen, but on the other hand, he was communicating (mostly by writing on a white board), and we thought that if they could get the lung problem under control, we would

---

when faced with new information that forced him to question his earlier assumptions and that required him to face some really bad news, he still believed with all of his heart that Hashem was in control and everything was for the best. He never once had the arrogance to think that he had figured it all out. His *bitachon* was absolute and unwavering.

have more time to figure out what the results of the CT meant and how to deal with that.

After the meeting, the oncologist, the social worker, and I went into the room to talk to Ely about the situation. In a gentle way, they explained how things could go from here. They told him that his breathing might improve over the next few hours or it might not. It actually brings a smile to my face when I remember how he reacted to this. He pulled out his white board, asked a few questions, stated his wishes, and then drew a graph. The graph looked something like this:

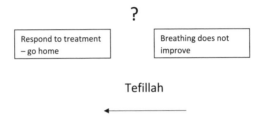

Even during this critical moment, which it turned out was his last communicative day, he was able to think both logically and deeply at the same time. He understood that the outcome was not yet clear—and perhaps not yet determined. And the thing that came to him clearly at that moment was the need for and the power of *tefillah*.

After they left, I told him that family members would be coming to be with him just in case things went downhill. From that time on, he seemed relaxed and at ease, and he seemed to enjoy every single interaction that he had with all of the loved ones who came to visit. He smiled as each child (including stepchildren) and his parents and brother came to spend time with him. He enjoyed some very special moments with his daughters as they sang the songs he loved. He hugged Tamar, and he gently touched each person who came to be with him. He left everyone with an image of him smiling and calmly accepting the love that we were giving him.

On May 15, 2019, 10 Iyar 5779, in the early morning hours, Ely peacefully stopped breathing. He was not in pain, and I was with him while he left this world.

Chapter 18

Hashem's Decree Is Upon Us

It is hard to believe after everything we went through that this was the final result of this chapter in our lives. A few weeks after Ely passed away, in conversation with a friend, I told her that this is the first time in my life I can remember that the answer to my prayers was a final, resounding NO. This was truly shocking to me, since in the past, if the things I prayed for did not come through, there was still hope that they might in the future.

Here, there was a final answer—and it was not the one we were all praying for.

MAY 21, 2019/ 16 IYAR 5779

> Last Day of Shivah
> Today is the last day of shivah. I am looking at the *ner neshamah*, and remembering that Ely's *neshamah* is still with us. Here are some good thoughts in the midst of the sorrow.
> The moment of death was a moment of *kedushah*. I was there with him, and we experienced it together, in a way. I will never forget it. And it gave me strength for the funeral, when the body was just a body.

I feel very blessed to have had this unbelievable experience of a very special relationship with a very special person. Most people are not *zocheh* to this in an entire lifetime.

I will miss him so deeply, but he left so much behind. Writings, recordings, memories, life lessons, and of course, his dear children and grandchildren.

MAY 23, 2019/ 18 IYAR 5779

Post-Shivah

I first want to describe what I am feeling today. I am walking around with what feels like a heavy brick on my chest. Every once in a while, something sets me off and I start to cry. This morning, it happened when I passed the area that we used to walk through on our slow walks during treatment. It happened again as I was folding laundry. It takes me by surprise, since when I am not crying, I am somewhat functional most of the time. I was able to work on the *matzeivah*, housework, and some errands. But most of the time, the grief is there—alive and well.

"It's not fair." "It shouldn't be this way." "He was too young." Statements like these really rub me the wrong way. True, I really, really wish that this was not the reality. But since it is, I have no doubt that this is what is supposed to be. Nothing is random. Actually, the very fact that this was so unexpected, so unusual, reminds me that it is supernatural. Why do we think that only things that we perceive as "good" come from Hashem? Do we not believe that Hashem created the *entire* world? Including good and bad? Including life and death? How arrogant it is to say that something that God decided is not fair—or worse, wrong. Before an event happens, we have the right to argue with God. We can ask for things to be different. But once the final verdict is here, who are we to judge the Ultimate Judge? Again, I emphasize that I believe that God is good—and it is we who are limited in our understanding.

The other thing that is helping me is the realization that time is one thing from our perspective but another thing altogether in reality. There is no doubt in my mind that the time that Ely had in this world cannot be measured in minutes and seconds, but rather in deeds and living.

I want to coin a new term: life-minutes.

A life-minute is a minute spent in meaningful existence, and is completely different than a regular minute, which is just time itself. A life-minute may be spent in loving someone else, thinking about higher level things, performing mitzvot, improving yourself, contributing to the world, or any other thing that has true meaning. In life-minutes, Ely lived a very, very long life. Similarly, our years together may have been short in dry terms, but in life-minutes, we had a very, very long time together.

I am thankful for having been *zocheh* to have such a special relationship with such a special person. It was a gift that will always be cherished. I wish that we could have continued to live together in this world for many more years, but I understand that that was not the plan. And I believe deep down that we will be reunited again in some form. My loss is vast and deep. But my comfort is in trusting God and in being thankful. That has not changed.

MAY 24, 2019/ 19 IYAR 5779

Lonely Grief

Despite people saying the "right" things, nothing right now is comforting. Why? Well, of course there's just the enormity of the loss, and nothing that anyone says can change that.

But it's more than that. When people say, "We are sorry for your loss," "We're here for you," or other such things, they are talking about a generic story. They are talking to someone who lost her husband, perhaps like other people who have lost a spouse. But they are not talking about losing *Ely*. They are not able to connect to the person that he was, and the enormous loss of this full person. They don't understand that my *neshamah* is grieving for his *neshamah*. They don't understand how connected we were, and how unthinkable it is to live without *him*. Not without a "husband" in some generic sense. But *him*. The person that he was. It is impossible to describe this, but it is a very lonely feeling.

Even if I were to join a support group of other women who lost their husbands, or if I were to confide in a close friend, or if I were to describe what I am going through, there is a vast loneliness that I am feeling. Nobody has ever or will ever experience what I am experiencing, because nobody ever lost *Ely* in the *particular way* that I have. The best I can do is to surround myself with people who care about me and love me and people who cared about him and loved him. But unfortunately, that just doesn't get to the heart of the matter. Because the only person who would be able to *really* understand what I am going through right now is Ely.

But that brings me to a thought. I do believe that there is something that can help. I think that learning about the *neshamah*, or being connected in a spiritual way to a higher level, perhaps connecting to Hashem through *tefillah*, those are things that can help me right now. Because it is on that level that the loss and the feelings are being experienced.

There is actually something achingly beautiful about feeling this loneliness and grief. There was a time in my life when I was not able to feel anything, and it happened to be the time that I was least connected to my inner self. That is another story for another time, but the very strong feelings that I am experiencing right now are directly a result of my human connection. They are straight from the *neshamah*. So as I am writing, it occurs to me that at this time—*davka* at this time—I potentially can connect to Hashem at a much deeper level. Through my pain, my *neshamah* is coming to the surface, and it is through my *neshamah* that I am able to connect. I think that this is the true way to alleviate my loneliness, and that thought does give me comfort.[1]

JUNE 3, 2019/ 29 IYAR 5779

Points of Comfort

There are two additional things that have provided some comfort during this painful time. The first is the realization that Ely came into my life to teach me. I always felt that this was true; during our time together we really underwent tremendous growth and development. He was always at least a few steps ahead of me, and I truly learned from him. I believe that I have internalized so much of what he taught me, and I hope to carry that forward in my life.

The second is that I realized that this world is for working, for growing, for trying to make sure our *neshamah* leads our body and not the other way around. I read a piece this morning in *Derech Hashem*,[2] which stated that the time for working is limited and the time for reward (i.e., *Olam Haba*, the afterlife) is unlimited. So I realized that Ely really had achieved a very high level in his life, and Hashem decided that he had done enough work. If his *neshamah* is now enjoying the rewards of a life well-lived, then I can be more at peace with the fact that he is not here.

We here on earth are suffering from his death.

He is not.

And as he would undoubtedly tell us, our suffering is for a higher purpose—to move us closer to God. It is our choice to use it in this way, and I think that if we do, we will be honoring his memory in the best way possible.

Yehi zichro baruch—יהי זכרו ברוך.

---

1   In reality, I still found it difficult to connect—it was too painful most of the time. It was comforting, though, to learn more about the spiritual side of things. I found that about two months after Ely passed away, I was sometimes able to daven in a real way, but that when I did, I inevitably cried. I think it was because when my *neshamah* was exposed, I was vulnerable.

2   A book by Rabbi Moshe Chaim Luzzatto, which delves into many spiritual principles of how Hashem runs the world.

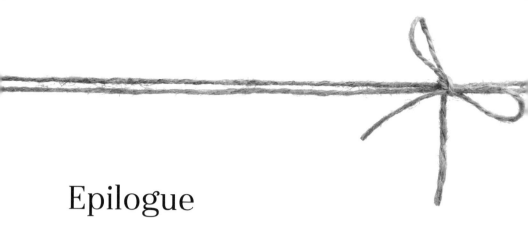

Epilogue

It is now the month of Elul. We are gearing up for Rosh Hashanah and Yom Kippur, and what is hitting me is that it is hard to believe that last year at this time we had not even a hint of what was to come during the year. Every year, we pray that the coming year will be a good one for us and our families. I think that in the back of my mind, I always just assumed that it would be a good year—maybe with some ups and downs—but I never would have imagined this.

Reflecting back on the last four months since Ely passed away, I am surprised by the intensity of the grief and by my inability sometimes to grab onto the bigger picture.

The most difficult part for me is a deep, existential loneliness. This is not the same thing as being by myself. Of equal intensity is the sadness I feel for our daughter Tamar, who has lost her father at such a young age.

There a few things that give me comfort.

- The most comforting thing for me has been working on this book.
- Learning Torah, and specifically in the realm of deeper things such as life purpose (books, videos and *shiurim* on Jewish thought), is like a balm for my soul.
- Seeing my children—and remembering both the gifts that God gave me and the job that He gave me—gives me strength.
- A few select people have really been able to give me comfort.

I also have a few insights:

- There is no choice now but to fly. It's either that or sink down. The stakes are high.
- I have seen that sources of comfort do come my way. I believe that Hashem will continue to guide me through this, and I pray that He continues to send me these sources of comfort.
- I thank God for the ability to cry.
- I know that the traumatic events of the last ten months, from the time that Ely was diagnosed until now, have had a profound effect on me.

It is Elul—a time for reflection, introspection, and improvement. Over the last four months since Ely passed away, I have had a few moments of clarity and many moments of pain. Sometimes they happen together. But more often, I try to bury the pain and at those times, I forget the lessons I have learned, I forget to turn to Hashem, and I forget how to move forward with the jobs I have to do in the world. I feel that I have a responsibility now to help ensure that Ely's presence in this world and the messages that he had to offer continue to live on.

He often said that by getting sick, he had credibility in his messages—he wasn't just talking theoretically. Well, since his devotion did not waver even in the face of death, his credibility and the message he had to give the world is even stronger. I now feel that in some way which I can't explain, his death was a *kiddush Hashem*, and it is up to me to actualize this. He did his part. I now have to do my part.

So that is the burden and the blessing that I have been carrying around with me.

I have begun to see beauty again. It is achingly beautiful, this world. The morning breeze. The flowers. The people walking by. A child waves to me with a huge innocent smile on her face, and I am touched. I can't explain why I suddenly woke up to all of this again. But perhaps my heart is now a little less afraid to open up to the world.

This morning, my *tefillah* was also better than it has been.

For a moment, I felt a real connection. I think that our emotions are the key to our connection with God. The fact that God created emotions is a wonder in and of itself. Where do these feelings come from? I am truly thankful that we have feelings. And that is a good place to be, considering that the predominant feeling I have had over the last few months is pain. I still have pain, but somehow, through the pain, I am also experiencing now a certain positive sensation as well.

I have been able to listen to music again.

I have been connecting to the prayers of this time period.

I am dreading Rosh Hashanah on the one hand. But on the other hand, maybe it will be cathartic. Maybe this year, instead of asking for specific things, I will just try to connect. To cry out. To feel Hashem's love.

Rage

Wow, that surprised me. I am not an angry person. In fact, I was convinced that the "anger phase" of grief would not apply to me. And indeed it hadn't for the most part. Last week, I met with my coaching mentor, and we had a really good talk. Surprisingly, she informed me that indeed I am angry, even if I don't think I'm feeling anger. This was based on something that I had said, but even though I very much respect her ability to read people, I didn't fully believe her.

Until yesterday.

I had two clues while on the road, but I didn't put it together until later. I was driving along, on my way to an appointment, when two cars ahead of me, a man stopped his car in the middle of the street, and in a rage stomped over to another car which was on the side of the road and tried to open the driver's door. I did not see what had happened that led to this action, but I sat there in my car, watching apprehensively, as he managed to pry the other car's door open and somehow got ahold of what looked like a stick of some sort. A few men from other cars jumped up and held him back, and the incident quieted down. The rage on this man's face and in his body language was quite frightening. It took me a few minutes to equilibrate, and then I continued on my way, but the scene stayed with me.

On my way home, something else happened that I didn't quite put together until later. As I was turning off the main road to head toward Modiin, I noticed that at the bus stop just past the traffic light where I was turning, there was police activity and many security cars surrounding the bus stop. I didn't think too much of it other than relief that I was turning off the road at that point. Later, I saw a headline that there had been a stabbing at a bus stop just outside of Modiin. Thank God, the victim was only lightly injured, and they caught the perpetrator, but when I realized that that must have happened just where I made my turn, I was in shock.

I immediately connected these two incidents in my mind: two scenes of human rage that I was very close to within a very short period of time. I thought to myself, *Wow, there must be a message here for me. Let me try to figure this out.* Then I remembered that I was feeling a kernel of anger inside of me toward someone that I perceived as having potentially harmed a particular relationship. I took these incidents on the road as a sign that I needed to recognize and deal with the anger that I was feeling. I did a bit of soul searching and thought that I had managed it OK.

This morning, it became apparent that I had not yet gotten to the depth of my feelings. My daughter Tamar was giving me a very hard time. She didn't want to go to school. Knowing that she too is grieving, I tried my best to be sympathetic without giving in to her demands. After a while, when nothing seemed to be working, and she had dug in her heels deeper than ever, my anger started to build up. I knew that she was touching upon some raw nerve, but I didn't really understand it and couldn't control it. So I burst out in anger, yelling at her—after I had promised myself that I would not lose it. She of course started crying, and both of us had to remove ourselves from the situation for a few minutes. After we both calmed down, we were able to talk, and the entire mood shifted. Finally, she went to school (happily, even), and I was left alone with my thoughts, sitting in my car.

Here's where it got interesting. I found myself so angry with the situation: Why do I have to deal with all of these difficult things at a time like this? I felt a surge of rage building up inside of me, and before

I knew it, sounds were coming out from a deep place in my body. It is hard to describe what it must have sounded like, but I am guessing that the closest thing would be a wounded animal. I shocked myself. I had never ever in my life felt this thing, this rage. I didn't even know what that emotion was until that moment. I also can't tell you who I was angry at. I just know that it was something I had never felt in my life. And then I realized that this thing called grief is something that is unpredictable and certainly not logical. It brings out emotions that I never knew existed, and it comes at random times. I thought back to the man that had exhibited road rage yesterday, and I felt sorry for him that he must be very familiar with this emotion.

In a weird way, I am glad I experienced that. I had this moment of lucidity afterwards, where I understood that part of this whole experience is meant to bring me to extreme moments of feeling. For some reason, I must know what it is like to experience these extremes. I know that rage and anger are not a prominent part of my personality, and I am glad that that is true. But I am also somewhat glad to see that I have the capacity for a whole range of emotions that I had not recognized before. A strangely comforting thought.

The Power of Emotion

I am beginning to understand that emotion is the key to our lives and to connecting to God.

Emotion is an inexplicable but undeniable part of our existence. To me, right now, it is the greatest testament to God, and it is what allows us to touch the edges of feeling Godliness in the world.

The real tragedy is when there is no emotion. I would rather feel deep pain than nothing at all. I have learned that over the years. And Hashem has given us that as a tool. It helps us know when we are going in the wrong direction (e.g., by feeling guilt and shame) and when we are on track. The more we tune in, the more intuitive we can become.

I think I now have a heightened sense of emotion and intuition. I am not sure I can always interpret what I am feeling correctly, but the depth of the feeling and the awareness has definitely increased. I can't explain this. But I am thankful for it. I think it may be a gift from God that is allowing me to have some measure of comfort during this time. But it is clear that I have to allow it to be—and to recognize that it is from God.

I have a sense that this time in my life, although lonely and difficult, is critical for me to be able to do whatever it is that I am supposed to do in this world. I can hear Ely explaining this to me. I can imagine sitting across from him, sipping a good cup of coffee and discussing the issue. I am learning to have these conversations on my own.

I think that God has singled us out for some task. That is true for everyone, but I am becoming more and more aware of it for me. And one of the lessons that I have learned through this ordeal is that it is critical that I try to figure it out to the best of my ability, and to follow the signs. But I will not necessarily be able to know exactly what it is, and it will probably be dynamic. As I am writing these words, I am wondering if this is part of my job. It feels like it is.

Our *rav* gave a *shiur* a couple of weeks ago on Rav Kook's *Orot Hateshuvah*. Rav Kook stresses looking inside ourselves, connecting to our unique role in the world, and finding the right way of connecting to God from a positive point.

This resonates with me right now. How can I dig deeper and find the right spot? When I hear the shofar this year, will I be able to feel it in my gut? Do I need to define what it is that I am feeling? One thing is for sure: I plan to bring a whole pack of tissues with me.

Faith

Faith is not something you can capture in a word or a sentence. It is an evolving entity, which takes different forms at different times. Sometimes you might think you have it figured out, but then it comes at you from a different angle, a different layer, a different perspective. I also realized that it is helpful to remember that there is the cognitive part and the emotional part, and those two sections don't always match up. For me, the cognitive part is usually easier. Because I really do believe, as I've expressed many times, that God is in charge and that He is good. Even now, in the midst of my sorrow, I believe that there was a purpose to what happened, and that ultimately it is for the best. If I hear other people questioning that, I actually get upset, because I know with all of my being that it is true. But the question I am asking myself is: Do I **feel** it?

Do I feel it to the point that I can thank God for what has happened? That is a lot to ask. I am not sure I am ready for that. Does that mean that I don't believe that it is for the best? No. I do believe it, but I strive to really feel it.

My emotions have definitely taken a more central role than they did in the past. Emotions can be unpredictable, surprising, and don't follow a straight or logical path. For me, that is difficult to cope with, because I like knowing what to expect. But one thing I have learned through this is that letting go, depending on God to lead us, and being patient in our understanding of the world and our role in it allows for beauty to seep in. There is beauty in the unexpected, even when it is intertwined with pain.

I recall the following passage from Ely's journal, written at a time when he saw and felt that God was leading us down this path:

> *Occasionally, we may glimpse hints of the great orchestration behind these seemingly random coincidences. An orchestra does not play beautiful music through random sounds from each instrument; it depends highly on the organized structure of the musical score and the skills of the conductor to manage its execution. We appreciate through insights like we had today that the world is orchestrated in a beautiful way as well.*

But what about the fact that he died? Does it still mean that the world is beautiful and orchestrated?

The absolute and unequivocal answer is yes. I know that I and the rest of Ely's loved ones are still in the very early, fresh pain of losing him. But I know that he would say: Hashem is with you, even in your pain. There is tremendous love—you just have to open your heart to it.

I have found that the things that give me the most comfort are the things that touch my soul. Even if they make me cry—and sometimes because they do.

So I cry a lot now. Sometimes it is from pain and loneliness, sometimes it is from kindness from another person, sometimes it is from a deep thought or idea, and sometimes from frustration. But always, always, is it a testament to being alive. And being alive means being connected to God. So in that sense, Ely is more alive than ever.

ואתם הדבקים בה' אלוקיכם
חיים כולכם היום.

(דברים ד:ד)

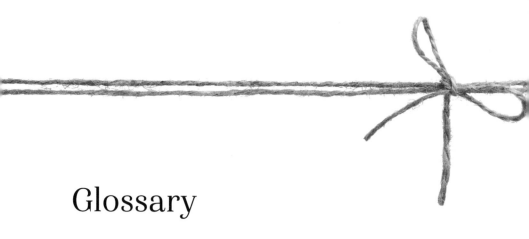

Glossary

ahavat Hashem: love of God.

Al Hanisim: lit., "for the miracles"; a special prayer said on Chanukah and Purim.

Amidah: the silent prayer, recited while standing in place.

Am Yisrael: the People of Israel.

anavah: modesty, humbleness.

ani ma'amin: I believe.

avodat Hashem: service of God.

baruch Hashem: Thank God.

Beit Hamikdash: the Holy Temple.

b'ezrat Hashem: with God's help; God willing.

Birkat Hamazon: Grace after Meals.

bitachon: trust.

berachah (pl.–berachot): blessing(s).

chag: holiday.

chametz: leavened bread.

chanukiyah: menorah.

chessed: lovingkindness.

chizuk: strength.

Chumash: one of the Five Books of the Torah, not in scroll form.

dati: religious; observant.

daven: pray.

David Hamelech: King David.

davka: specifically.

Dayeinu: lit., "it would have been enough"; a song from the Passover Haggadah praising God for every step of the salvation.

Eishet Chayil: lit., "a woman of valor"; song from Proverbs 31, sung on Friday night.

emunah: faith.

Eretz Yisrael: Land of Israel.

eved Hashem: servant of God.

Ezrat Avoteinu: lit., "the help of our fathers"; prayer said before the silent prayer.

galut: exile.

geulah: redemption.

haftarah: portion from Prophets that is read after the Torah portion on Shabbat.

Har Habayit: Temple Mount.

Hashem: lit., the name; God.

hashgachah/hashgachah pratit: Divine providence.

Havdalah: lit., separation; a prayer said immediately after Shabbat.

Iyov: Job.

kavanah: directed concentration; intention.

kedushah: holiness.

Kiddush: the prayer said over wine before the night and day Shabbat meals.

kiddush Hashem: sanctification of God's name.

Kotel: Western Wall.

Maariv: the evening prayers.

matzeivah: a gravestone.

mesirut nefesh: complete giving of oneself.

Mi Sheberach: the prayer for the sick.

mitzvah (pl.–mitzvot): commandment(s) from the Torah.

ner neshamah: a candle lit in memory of the deceased.

neshamah: soul.

Olam Haba: the afterlife; the World to Come.

rav (pl.–rabbanim): rabbi(s).

refuah sheleimah: a complete recovery or healing; in prayer, it is often followed by the name of a specific person.

Rosh Chodesh: the first day of the new lunar month.

seudah: a festive meal.

seudah shlishit: the third meal of Shabbat.

Shacharit: the morning prayers.

Shalom Aleichem: lit., "May peace be with you"; a song sung on Friday night welcoming the Shabbat angels.

shiurim: Torah lessons.

shlichim: messengers.

shul: synagogue.

siddur: a prayer book.

tefillah (pl.–tefillot): prayer(s).

tefillin: phylacteries.

Tehillim: Psalms.

teshuvah: repentance.

tikkun: corrective action.

tzaddik (pl.–tzaddikim): righteous person(s).

Yad Hashem: the Hand of God.

yetzer hara: the evil inclination.

yetziat Mitzrayim: the Exodus from Egypt.

yehi zichro baruch: "May his memory be blessed."

yirat Hashem: fear of God.

zocheh: to be worthy; to merit.

About the Authors

RICKI SIMON is a patent agent specializing in medical devices, as well as a life coach with a focus on Jewish perspectives on coping and overcoming challenges. She received a bachelor's degree from Stern College with a dual major in Jewish Studies and Biophysical Sciences, and then went on to study biomedical engineering at Rutgers University. In recent years, she has focused on learning Jewish texts related to self-improvement and spiritual development. Ricki made aliyah in 2000, and lives in Modiin with her family.

DR. ELY SIMON, *z"l*, was a neurologist, neuroscientist, and biomedical engineer, who was both a hands-on clinician as well as a serial entrepreneur in the field of digital medicine. After receiving degrees in electrical engineering from Columbia University, and in medicine and biomedical engineering from Case Western Reserve University, he completed a residency in neurology. Before moving to Israel, Dr. Simon was a Senior Research Fellow at the Laboratory of Neural Control at the National Institutes of Health (NIH). Dr. Simon made aliyah in 1996 and practiced neurology at Ichilov Hospital in Tel Aviv. He launched a company, NeuroTrax, for computerized cognitive assessment, as well as a company for managing migraine pain, and was in the planning stages of opening a brain health center for integrated care. In addition to publishing over fifty journal articles in the fields of neurology, physiology, and behavioral medicine, Dr. Simon was also very interested in the study of human emotion, self-improvement, and spirituality from a Jewish perspective and the integration of these disciplines into medicine and science.